Sustainable Transport

ISSUES

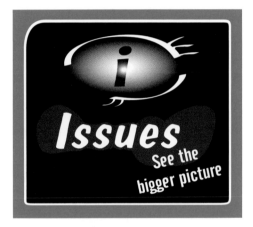

Volume 200

Series Editor

Lisa Firth

Independence

Educational Publishers

Cambridge

First published by Independence

The Studio, High Green

Great Shelford

Cambridge CB22 5EG

England

© Independence 2011

Photocopy licence

The material in this book is protected by copyright. However, the
purchaser is free to make multiple copies of particular articles for instructional
purposes for immediate use within the purchasing institution.
Making copies of the entire book is not permitted.

British Library Cataloguing in Publication Data

Sustainable transport. -- (Issues ; v. 200)

1. Transportation--Great Britain. 2. Transportation--

Environmental aspects--Great Britain. 3. Transportation

and state--Great Britain.

I. Series II. Firth, Lisa.

388'.0941-dc22

ISBN-13: 978 1 86168 572 8

Printed in Great Britain
MWL Print Group Ltd

CONTENTS

Chapter 1 Transport Trends

Chapter 2 Transport and Environment

OTHER TITLES IN THE ISSUES SERIES

For more on these titles, visit: www.independence.co.uk

A note on critical evaluation

Because the information reprinted here is from a number of different sources, readers should bear in mind the origin of the text and whether the source is likely to have a particular bias when presenting information (just as they would if undertaking their own research). It is hoped that, as you read about the many aspects of the issues explored in this book, you will critically evaluate the information presented. It is important that you decide whether you are being presented with facts or opinions. Does the writer give a biased or an unbiased report? If an opinion is being expressed, do you agree with the writer?

Sustainable Transport offers a useful starting point for those who need convenient access to information about the many issues involved. However, it is only a starting point. Following each article is a URL to the relevant organisation's website, which you may wish to visit for further information.

Transport

Information from Keep Britain Tidy.

Our growing use of cars has a variety of environmental, social and health consequences. Some are highly visible and directly relevant to everyday life. For example, accident statistics show that our roads are dangerous, while traffic congestion has adverse effects on our health and wellbeing. Other impacts are less immediately obvious but no less important. For example, the gases and chemicals released by engines make a large contribution to global warming and air pollution. Indeed, climate change is fast becoming the greatest challenge we face in the coming century.

The more we use cars, the more the air becomes polluted. Exhaust fumes contain carbon monoxide, oxides of nitrogen, volatile organic compounds and particulates, all of which are harmful to health when released into the atmosphere. Soot particles cause lung damage, especially when they contain chemicals such as benzine.

Increasing amounts of urban traffic – partly caused by greater distances between home and places of work – have created fear of traffic. Because people feel less vulnerable driving compared with walking or cycling, more and more trips are being made by car. The resulting lack of exercise can cause problems for health and overall fitness.

⇨ On average, one in seven children suffers from asthma; this figure increases to one in three in inner city areas.

⇨ In slow-moving traffic, pollution levels are higher inside cars than outside.

⇨ Cycling or walking briskly for half an hour a day can halve the risk of heart disease.

**YoungTransNet surveys show that many young people would like to travel in a more sustainable way, with 30% of them saying they would like to cycle to school**

Sustainable transport is any means of transport which reduces fuel consumption, pollution and car use. This includes cycling, rail and bus transport, walking or even travelling by scooter.

Transport and schools

Young children today have far less freedom than their parents had at the same age. Fear of traffic and stranger danger, combined with the overall increase in general car use and ownership are leading to an increasing number of parents taking their children to school in the car. This has a number of consequences for pupils and staff, particularly in terms of pupil health and wellbeing.

Walking and cycling are excellent forms of physical activity and the journey to school can make an important contribution to increasing these activity levels. Patterns of activity are set in early childhood, so early lack of exercise can lead to a higher risk of future obesity, high blood pressure, poor psychological wellbeing and coronary heart disease. Walking and cycling can help

KEEP BRITAIN TIDY

children to gain confidence and make friends, helping both to increase independence and traffic sense. Current research also suggests that more-active children arrive at school more alert and focused and achieve better academic results.

YoungTransNet surveys show that many young people would like to travel in a more sustainable way, with 30% of them saying they would like to cycle to school. Statistics from the Department for Transport, however, show that currently only 1% of them do. Surveys also show that over half of all primary pupils live within a mile of their school, yet one-third are driven there.

Safe Routes to Schools (SRS) projects, run by the national organisation Sustrans, are a good way for pupils to consider alternative forms of travel and help improve access to the school for walkers and cyclists. The projects encourage and enable children to walk and cycle to school through a combined package of practical and educational measures, to:

⇨ improve road safety and reduce child casualties;

⇨ improve children's health and development;

⇨ reduce traffic congestion and pollution.

SRS projects are child-centred. They build on small steps to raise awareness and change travel behaviour and benefit the whole local community by helping to create safer, healthier environments.

National Curriculum links with transport can be made in English, maths, ICT, science, design & technology, art and design as well as literacy and numeracy. The geography curriculum makes specific reference to road traffic, road safety and sustainability.

Each school is different, with its own local problems and possible solutions. Developing a school travel plan can help ensure the complete situation is considered and that appropriate action is taken. All local authorities have Local Transport Plan funding for Safe Routes to Schools, road safety training and education campaigns. There will also be a local school travel advisor who can offer help and guidance.

School travel plans

Schools can meet the main requirements of the Eco-Schools transport theme by drawing up a school travel plan. A school travel plan is a package of ideas and actions drawn up by the school community to promote more safe walking, cycling and shared transport to and from school. In developing a travel plan, school communities show a commitment to promote sustainable travel.

Using a school travel plan, children, parents and school staff are encouraged to think about the environment and lead fitter and healthier lifestyles, through the promotion of Walk to School campaigns, using children's long-term walking incentive schemes such as the excellent WOW (Walk On Wednesday scheme), and through the promotion of cycle training and the National Bike Week campaign. More information on School Travel Plans can be found on the Sustrans website

Further information

For useful information, practical advice and lesson ideas surrounding the theme of walking to school, visit the Walk to School campaign website. The Walk to School campaign is run by national charity Living Streets, and aims to encourage all parents and children to make walking to school part of their daily routine. The campaign has existed since 1995, and reaches over two million children each year. The campaign consists of two awareness events (Walk to School Week in May, and Walk to School Month, October) and a year-round walking promotion scheme called WoW (Walk Once a Week).

For examples of how Eco-Schools have tackled transport issues visit the Case Studies section of the Eco-Schools website (www.eco-schools.org.uk). In particular read how Millfield Primary School in Norfolk developed a sustainable transport project called Stamp Stanley, which was voted European winner in the Toyota Environment and Innovation competition in 2007. The Links and Resources section of the site also provides details of organisations that will be able to offer your school help on transport issues.

⇨ The above information is from Keep Britain Tidy's Eco-Schools programme and is reproduced with permission from Sustrans. Visit www.eco-schools.org.uk for more.

© Keep Britain Tidy

Use of public transport

Public Transport Statistics Bulletin Great Britain: 2009 Edition.

The Department for Transport has published national statistics on public transport in *Public Transport Statistics Bulletin: Great Britain 2009 Edition* according to the arrangements approved by the UK Statistics Authority.

The key points are as follows:

⇨ Between 2007/08 and 2008/09, passenger journeys on local buses in England are provisionally estimated to have increased by 1.6 per cent to 4,783 million journeys. This was mainly driven by an increase in bus patronage in London of 2.8 per cent with passenger journeys in the rest of England increasing by 0.5 per cent.

⇨ Over the same period, passenger journeys on trams and light rail systems in England increased by 1.3 per cent.

⇨ Bus patronage largely remained unchanged in Scotland and Wales between the two years.

Between 2007/08 and 2008/09, passenger journeys on local buses in England are provisionally estimated to have increased by 1.6 per cent to 4,783 million journeys

⇨ In 2008/09 local bus operators ran 99.0 per cent of their scheduled mileage, unchanged from 2007/08. The target for 2010/11 is 99.5 per cent.

⇨ Average local bus fares in Great Britain increased by two per cent at constant prices (i.e. allowing for inflation) between 2007/08 and 2008/09.

⇨ The average rating for overall satisfaction for bus services in England is 82, unchanged from 2007/08. Overall satisfaction is higher than this in both metropolitan and non-metropolitan areas at 84 points out of 100. In London this rating is lower at 80 points, although both London and metropolitan areas have shown an increase of one point over the year. The score for non-metropolitan areas is unchanged from the previous year.

⇨ The upward trend in passenger journeys on the National Rail network continued with 1,274 million passenger journeys made in 2008/09, an increase

of three per cent on 2007/08. Passenger kilometres travelled on national rail increased by 3.9 per cent to 50.7 billion in 2008/09.

⇨ London Underground passenger kilometres increased to 8.6 billion in 2008/09, up four per cent compared with 2007/08.

Average local bus fares in Great Britain increased by two per cent... between 2007/08 and 2008/09

DfT is currently undertaking a methodological review of its Public Service Vehicle survey. The estimates of bus patronage for 2007/08 and 2008/09 are based on a new estimation methodology and are provisional. Trends between the two years should be interpreted with care and comparisons with previous years will be distorted until prior years are revised.

29 October 2009

⇨ Information from the Department for Transport. Visit www.dft.gov.uk for more information.

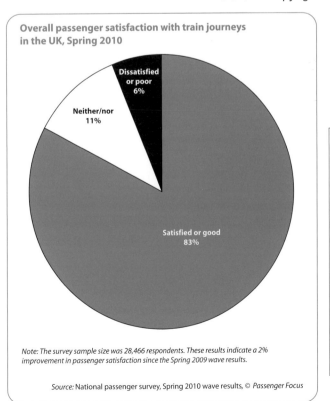

Overall passenger satisfaction with train journeys in the UK, Spring 2010

Dissatisfied or poor 6%

Neither/nor 11%

Satisfied or good 83%

Note: The survey sample size was 28,466 respondents. These results indicate a 2% improvement in passenger satisfaction since the Spring 2009 wave results.

Source: National passenger survey, Spring 2010 wave results, © Passenger Focus

DEPARTMENT FOR TRANSPORT

Motorway phobia

UK motorists drive 600 million miles to avoid motorways.

Just how far will anxious drivers go to avoid joining the motorway? More than 600 million miles, if the last year is anything to go by.

During that time UK drivers used the AA's online Route Planner to devise more than five million routes specifically to steer clear of motorways. The routes, weaving under, over and alongside busy multi-lane roads, averaged over 125 miles each. Stretched end-to-end they would extend around the world 24,000 times.

Though motorways are statistically the UK's safest roads, they are a source of fear for millions of drivers, including many who avoid them altogether. And, as families across Britain embark on another wave of holiday journeys, an AA/Populus survey[1] reveals that nearly one in ten AA members (9%) believe they would benefit from refresher or confidence training on motorway driving.

Comment

AA Driving School's head of driver development Mark Peacock says:

'There is much evidence that motorways are our most feared and avoided roads, yet statistically they are safer than other roads. By steering clear of them drivers not only face a longer, slower journey, but are potentially putting themselves at greater risk on A-roads.[2]

'With help, many find they can quickly overcome their fears. Tailored motorway tuition with a fully-qualified instructor can help drivers build the skills and confidence to make our motorway network work for them.'

Motorway fact file

⇨ Young drivers and women are by far the least confident on motorways, according to AA/Populus research. Only 44 per cent of those aged 18–24 and 44 per cent of women said they were confident driving on motorways. The figures were 65 per cent and 70 per cent respectively for drivers aged 55–64 and male drivers.[3]

⇨ Research suggests that in their first year of driving nearly 20 per cent of men and 40 per cent of women avoid motorways altogether. By the third year after passing the test, 11 per cent of men and 28 per cent of women did no motorway driving.[4]

⇨ Around five million routes a year generated by the AA's online Route Planner are for drivers who opt to plan their journey to deliberately avoid motorways.

⇨ Though motorways are statistically Britain's safest roads, new drivers are over-represented among accidents, with drivers aged 17–24 involved in more than a quarter of motorway accidents involving death or injury.[4]

⇨ Driving too slowly, not merging safely when joining the motorway and not observing safe following distances are the most commonly observed problems, according to AA Driving School instructors.

Overcoming motorway phobia

A 62-year-old London widow asked AA Driving School to help her tackle motorways. She had never driven on one in 22 years since passing her test as her late husband had always done the driving, and she was fast losing touch with friends who were a motorway-journey away. She started her lessons nervously, but speed was not her only worry – she insisted on doing her lessons in her own car lest her peers should see her in a driving school car. She has now successfully completed her training, regained her independence, and is literally on the road to restoring old friendships.

A taxi driver in Bolton refused all jobs involving motorway driving for 20 years after he witnessed a serious accident. He booked a motorway lesson and, after starting out at 45mph with a queue of traffic behind, gradually gained the confidence to travel at a suitable speed. Now he gladly accepts motorway jobs, his takings have increased, and he is so delighted he has referred three other drivers to his instructor for lessons.

Notes

1   AA/Populus panel survey of 12,231 AA members, 7–14 December 2009.

2   The 2009 EuroRAP survey found that 60 per cent of A-roads failed to rate as safe, and rated single-carriageway A-roads as Britain's most dangerous roads.

3   AA/Populus panel survey of 13,905 drivers, 2–8 June 2009.

4   *Young drivers – where and when they are unsafe: analysis of road accidents in Great Britain 2000-2006* (IAM Motoring Trust, August 2008.

20 August 2010

⇨ Information from the Automobile Association (AA). Visit www.theaa.com for more.

© *Automobile Association (www.theaa.com)*

Public attitudes towards road congestion

The Department for Transport has published the statistical report Public attitudes towards road congestion, November 2009 to February 2010 according to arrangements approved by the UK Statistics Authority.

This report discusses the combined results for questions included in the Office for National Statistics' (ONS) Opinions Omnibus Survey, and covers the following issues:

⇨ patterns and frequency of road use;

⇨ attitudes towards road congestion;

⇨ effectiveness and fairness of alternative road charging schemes.

Patterns and frequency of road use

⇨ The vast majority of car drivers, 88 per cent, said they used their car at least twice a week, with most of these saying they drove every day. Only 24 per cent of bus passengers reported that they travelled by bus with this frequency.

⇨ Motorway travel amongst car drivers is much less frequent, however, with less than one in five drivers saying they used these roads at least twice a week. Almost a quarter said they used motorways less than twice a year.

⇨ Adults' most frequent journeys occur mostly during 'peak' periods. As expected, this pattern is more pronounced for commuting journeys but smaller 'peaks' are still evident for other personal journeys, possibly related to school start and end times or shop opening hours.

⇨ Almost half of all adults who travel to and from work during 'peak' times said it would be easy for them to travel outside of these periods while a quarter said it would be impossible.

Attitudes towards road congestion

⇨ Over four in five adults thought that congestion was a serious problem in the country and nine in ten said that it was important for Government to tackle the problem, although both of these proportions have fallen slightly over the last two years.

The vast majority of car drivers, 88 per cent, said they used their car at least twice a week, with most of these saying they drove every day. Only 24 per cent of bus passengers reported that they travelled by bus with this frequency

⇨ Just under a quarter of adults said that congestion was a problem for the majority of their journeys, a similar level to two years ago but more than the proportion reported last year. Three in ten said that road congestion was rarely a problem for them.

⇨ Two-fifths of adults thought that congestion was rarely a problem for them on their most frequent journey, while a quarter thought that congestion was a problem for the majority of these journeys.

⇨ 66 per cent of adults said that congestion was worse in and around towns than on major routes although this percentage drops slightly for those who frequently use motorways.

⇨ A quarter of motorway users said they experienced motorway congestion on a majority of these journeys, an increase on the proportion reported last year, and three in ten said unreliable journey time was the main cause of their concern.

DEPARTMENT FOR TRANSPORT

Two in five motorway users said they routinely start their journey at different times to avoid congestion and over a third said they tend to take different routes or avoid motorways completely.

Effectiveness and fairness of alternative road charging schemes

⇨ Over half of adults agreed that the current system of paying for road use should change so that the amount people pay is based on how often, when and where they use the roads.

When asked whether they would be prepared to accept road pricing as long as there was no overall increase in the amount paid by motorists as a whole, 38 per cent agreed while 34 per cent disagreed

⇨ However, under a quarter thought that people driving on busy roads should pay more and a similar proportion said that people driving at busy times should pay more.

⇨ Three in ten adults thought that a new charging scheme based on times of travel and specific route taken would work in reducing congestion while over half said it would not.

⇨ Almost three in five of those who felt such a scheme wouldn't work gave people not being able to change their behaviour as a reason for this while a third said people wouldn't want to change.

⇨ 26 per cent of adults said that a new charging scheme based on these principles would be fair to road users, down from two years ago, while 55 per cent thought it would be unfair.

⇨ Again, the majority of those judging such a scheme to be unfair cited that people wouldn't be able to change their behaviour as a reason while over a third said the costs would be too much for some.

⇨ When asked whether they would be prepared to accept road pricing as long as there was no overall increase in the amount paid by motorists as a whole, 38 per cent agreed while 34 per cent disagreed. Two years ago, 41 per cent agreed and 35 per cent disagreed.

⇨ Almost half of adults said that money raised from such a scheme should be spent solely on roads and transport while over one in ten maintained that they didn't agree with it under any circumstances.

26 August 2010

⇨ The above information is reprinted with kind permission from the Department for Transport. Visit www.dft.gov.uk for more information on this and other related topics.

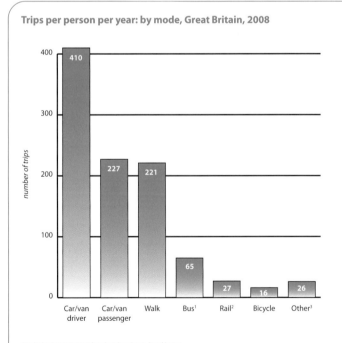

Trips per person per year: by mode, Great Britain, 2008

number of trips

Car/van driver	410
Car/van passenger	227
Walk	221
Bus[1]	65
Rail[2]	27
Bicycle	16
Other[3]	26

[1]Includes buses in London, local and non-local buses.
[2]Includes London Underground.
[3]Includes motorcycles, taxis and other private and public transport.

Average daily flow[1] of motor vehicles: by class of road[2] and year, Great Britain

flow in thousands.

Motorways
'A' roads – urban major roads
All major roads[3]
All 'A' roads
'A' roads – rural major roads
All roads
All minor roads

1965 1975 1985 1995 2005 2008

[1]Flow at an average point of each class of road.
[2]IMotorways include trunk motorways and principal motorways. Urban major roads include roads in built-up areas prior to 1995. Rural major roads include roads in non-built-up area prior to 1995.
[3]Includes all trunk and principal motorways and 'A' roads.

Source: Social trends 2010, Office for National Statistics, © Crown copyright

DEPARTMENT FOR TRANSPORT

The facts about road building

It's time to squash some myths about road building.

MYTH: We can build our way out of congestion

FACT: No, we can't. Road building just generates more traffic growth. New capacity makes journeys quicker in the short term, so people drive more often and even move further from work where houses are cheaper. Traffic also relocates from other congested roads. Traffic generation from new roads was studied for years and resulted in a landmark report by the Standing Advisory Committee on Trunk Road Assessment (SACTRA) called 'Trunk roads and the generation of traffic', HMSO, 1994. This is the only major study into trunk roads and traffic growth and concluded that new roads generate new traffic growth.

A major independent study into the impact of the Newbury bypass and two other road schemes showed that traffic levels predicted for 2010 in Newbury were already reached by 2003 – and that traffic had increased by almost 50% in that period. New development around the road was partially to blame for the increases.

MYTH: Drivers pay road tax so have a right to new roads

FACT: Roads are paid for out of general taxation and council tax. Motorists originally paid a 'road fund licence'

Future Roads

Bringing the traffic bottleneck closer to you.

which was ring-fenced to pay for road building and repair. However this was abolished in 1926, by then-Chancellor of the Exchequer Winston Churchill, who feared that the fund would lead to drivers feeling that they owned the road.

Modern 'road tax' – Vehicle Excise Duty – goes into general taxation. Roads are either paid for from council tax (in the case of smaller, local road schemes) or general taxation (for larger, regional and national schemes).

> *45% of drivers were willing and able to find other types of transport. Another 12% were able to use the car less, but unsure whether they were prepared to do so*

Pedestrians and cyclists therefore contribute just as much towards the cost of road building and maintenance as drivers.

MYTH: We have to use our cars

FACT: Not all car journeys are essential. Work by consultancy Transport for Quality of Life shows that 40% of journeys could be done by other means, another 40% could be changed if there was a small amount of investment, whilst only a 20% could not be done without a car.

Most journeys are short, even in rural areas, and could be done by cycling or walking. 23% of car journeys are less than two miles, which is less than a half-hour walk, or about a ten-minute bike ride.

We could also reduce the need to travel, by stopping the closure of small hospitals, shops and post offices – and improving rural buses would help people in the countryside get about without their cars. There's still plenty of scope for improvement!

MYTH: People love cars and won't give them up

FACT: Nearly half of Britain's drivers say they could already use their cars less often. The British Social Attitudes Survey, conducted annually since 1983, found that about 80% of people think the current level

of car use in the UK is having a serious, detrimental effect, and 66% say everyone should respond by using vehicles less often.

45% of drivers were willing and able to find other types of transport. Another 12% were able to use the car less, but unsure whether they were prepared to do so. And 18% were willing to cut back – but unable to do so for lack of public transport or safe routes for walking or cycling.

Most journeys are short, even in rural areas, and could be done by cycling or walking. 23% of car journeys are less than two miles, which is less than a half-hour walk, or about a ten-minute bike ride

MYTH: There are no alternatives to driving

FACT: We need more investment in the alternatives, but that won't happen if we pour money into road building. Interim results of the Sustainable Travel Towns pilot run by the Government and Sustrans have been a great success – reducing car use by over 10% and increasing levels of public transport use, walking and cycling. This is at a fraction of the cost of road building.

Car clubs are a great alternative to private car use, and can reduce car use by over 60%. Many short journeys could easily be walked or cycled, and investing in buses and trains would give more people alternatives to driving.

MYTH: More road capacity is necessary for the economy

FACT: Not according to the only major Government study into the economic benefits of road building. The impact of transport on the economy was studied by the Standing Advisory Committee on Trunk Road Assessment who reported in their 1999 SACTRA report that new roads are not necessary for economic growth: 'the empirical evidence of the scale and significance of [economic benefits from road building] is weak and disputed.'

The SACTRA report found that extra roads can even make poor areas worse as people and businesses use the new link to relocate or commute out. The Thames Gateway Bridge is an excellent example of this: the inspector rejected the bridge because it would bring lots of cars through poorer areas but do nothing to regenerate them.

12 May 2010

⇨ The above information is reprinted with kind permission from the Campaign for Better Transport. Visit www.bettertransport.org.uk for more information.

Responses to the question: 'To what extent would you support or oppose the introduction of a "pay as you go" system in which car and van drivers pay to use Britain's motorways and major roads based on the distance they travel: that is, charge per mile?'

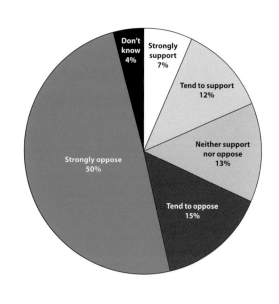

Source: Road use survey 2010, © Ipsos MORI

Responses to: 'To what extent do you agree with the following statement...*The introduction of a 'pay as you go' system on Britain's roads would make you think more about how much you drive?'*

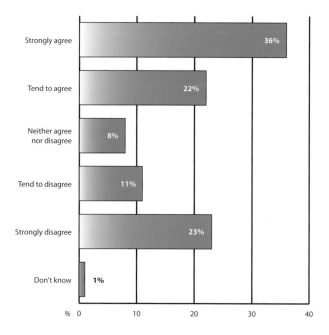

Governing and paying for England's roads

Executive summary of a report produced by the RAC Foundation.

By Stephen Glaister

The problem

The nation already has some of the most crowded roads in the world. Government expects a rise in population of 16% by 2033 and a return to economic growth. All indications are that traffic and congestion will increase.

Under the present system more expenditure on roads requires more funding from the Exchequer. Unless this is changed the general financial crisis will make it almost impossible to find resources to manage and cater for these growing needs.

> *Government expects a rise in population of 16% by 2033 and a return to economic growth. All indications are that traffic and congestion will increase*

Currently there is no direct relationship between the 'charges' paid by users – some £47 billion in 2009 – and the quantity and quality of what is provided in return. There are neither guaranteed standards of journey speed and reliability, nor compensation for delays incurred by the road-travelling public, which is common for other modes of transport.

There is also a striking lack of long-term, strategic thinking. Whilst the Government has established a systematic process of five-year plans for railways with an associated funding commitment (and private water companies are obligated to plan a quarter of a century in advance), there is nothing comparable for roads. It will be increasingly difficult for Government to justify this approach in the future.

The lack of long-term strategy and the inability to provide long-term funding cannot be adequately addressed within the present arrangements. Reform involves placing the road network at arm's length from government. This would remove roads policy from the cut and thrust of day-to-day politics and restore public trust in matters of road taxation and spending.

Scotland, Wales and Northern Ireland have devolved administrations. For simplicity, we restrict our attention to England.

The options range from relatively minor administrative reform to wholesale change. They include the establishment of:

⇨ a body within the government administration, but more autonomous than the present Highways Agency and with strategic duties; or

⇨ a legally separate public corporation or public trust. Whilst not privately owned this would have an independent board and powers to allocate budgets, make investment decisions and execute them; or

⇨ privately-owned utilities ('privatisation'). The assets are transferred by sale of shares to the public in for-profit companies, subject to independent regulation.

Reform might or might not involve the introduction of direct charges at the point of use ('tolls' or 'road user charging'). In this country direct charges are limited to a few bridges and the M6 Toll Road north of Birmingham, although they are commonplace in France, Italy and other countries. Currently some English roads (such as the M40) are provided and maintained under a system of shadow tolls, where a private contractor receives payment from Government which increases as more vehicles use them. This goes unseen by the road users and so does not influence their behaviour. Congestion problems could be greatly eased by replacing some of the present taxes with direct charges based on distance travelled. These might vary by time and place to reflect the local level of congestion. This would turn a current liability to HM Treasury into a financial asset.

But such a proposal for change must offer benefits for road users (the majority of the population) that are clear and credible or it will be rejected, as past governments have discovered. These benefits can include: lower fuel duty and road tax; better maintenance; better traffic regulation; removal of traffic pinch points enabling faster and more reliable journeys. A good package can offer effective management of existing congestion, new funding for road infrastructure and reductions in road taxation whilst maintaining the contribution to general government spending.

Any reform would need to ensure adequate protection of the public interest through appropriate legislation and regulation.

There are some things that the reform must avoid: transfer of ownership to asset managers who are incentivised to generate shareholder value by over-engineering; hiding undesirable cost savings by using

poor construction standards; transfer of ownership without an adequate, enforceable obligation to improve the service offered; creation of a body which has the responsibility to deliver all the required performance but has insufficient ability to fund these activities; a powerless consumer watchdog introduced as a gesture rather than as an effective complement to regulation; a mutually destructive relationship between the new body and regulators, national, regional and local government and road users; politicisation of the process; a confusion of objectives leading to inaction.

July 2010

⇨ The above information is an extract from the RAC Foundation's report *Governing and Paying for Britain's Roads*, and is reprinted with permission. Visit www.racfoundation.org for more information.

The road ahead: charging forward

Road pricing was once described as an 'economic no-brainer' because of the huge revenues it could generate for the Government and local authorities – however, the idea has many opponents, reports Richard Wray.

As Britain enters an age of austerity, the road network is already creaking in some places; Government and local authorities – which, after all are responsible for the bulk of the nation's roads – will need to look for ever more innovative ways of funding the creation of new roads and upkeep of existing routes.

'The fact is that motorists fund central coffers to the tune of £45bn a year through driving taxes,' says RAC motoring strategist Adrian Tink. 'Less than a quarter of that money is ploughed back into the roads. And for that, motorists are getting a very poor product.'

What a difference four years makes. In December 2006, the former boss of British Airways Sir Rod Eddington delivered a long-awaited report. The previous year, he had been asked by the Treasury and the Department for Transport (DfT) to produce a long-term strategy for the UK's transport infrastructure, with special reference to increasing the UK's productivity.

Intense pressure

Among his recommendations, Eddington came out strongly in favour of road pricing – various ways of charging for road use – describing it as 'an economic no-brainer' that could be worth up to £28bn a year by 2025. For local authorities, for many of whom roads are one of their largest assets, road pricing raises the tempting prospect of a new revenue stream that could augment council tax receipts, which are coming under intense pressure from central government.

Meanwhile, Tink is adamant that in reality, that prospect is grim: 'The chances of road pricing happening are next to zero. Politically it is a very toxic subject.' Following Eddington's report, almost two million people signed a petition on the No 10 website against road pricing.

Certainly the road haulage industry would kick up a major fuss if further charging were to be introduced. 'We pay enough already, thank you very much, so having to pay additional fees would be a very bitter pill to swallow,' says Road Haulage Association chief executive, Geoff Dunning.

Truck driver Paul McManus says: 'It's an utter disgrace that our livelihood is being taxed. Moving something from A to B is crucial to many businesses and adding an extra tax to moving goods is as good as effectively putting me out of business. Something needs to be done.'

The Government is also understood to be looking at ways of charging foreign haulage firms for the use of UK roads. A British truck doing about 100,000 miles a year contributes £30,000 in fuel duty to the UK Treasury. On the DfT's own reckoning, foreign-registered heavy goods vehicles pay just 0.008p a km – meaning the Treasury misses out on almost £250m in revenues every year.

Cost of upgrading

Foreign trucks travel an average of 649km a year in the UK, according to the DfT, arriving with an average of 760 litres of fuel and leaving with 480 litres but purchasing fewer than 10 litres in the UK. Some new British roads, meanwhile, are likely to be toll roads, but that will not cover the cost of upgrading existing infrastructure.

Some safety campaigners, meanwhile, have called for the creation of a transport regulator, involving both industry and road users, suggesting that such an independent body might also help improve the provision of funding. The Government, however, has played down the chance of that happening as there is already the DfT.

Matthew Lugg, chair of the UK Roads Board, believes that road pricing is inevitable at some stage. 'The current roads budget is £5bn. In the forthcoming spending review we are looking at between 25% and 50% cuts. We need to look at the current tax regime and how road maintenance is paid. If we don't receive adequate funding, with the increased levels of congestion on our roads in the future, we will compromise road safety.'

Can't afford to run a car?

Join the club of the 'pay as you drive'.

By Toby Walne

Buy a new petrol car today for £12,000 and, even if you don't drive a single mile, the first year of ownership will cost you £2,176 in depreciation, road tax and insurance, according to the AA. And if you drive 10,000 miles a year the costs including petrol, servicing and tyre wear will be £4,200. Over the past decade that figure has grown almost 40 per cent.

And last week, the latest rise in fuel duty kicked in, pushing up the price of petrol by 1p a litre.

It's little wonder that an alternative to vehicle ownership is proving more popular – the car club. Join one and you are spared the overheads and problems of having a car. Unlike traditional vehicle hire, club members 'pay as they drive' and have access to vehicles for periods as short as an hour. Members typically pay about £50 a year and between £5 and £10 an hour, depending on the car.

Annabel Dunstan, 44, a public relations manager from Oxford, sold her Renault people carrier three years ago in favour of car club Streetcar.

Annabel, who is married with children aged ten and 12, says: 'The car was a wasting asset just rusting away on the driveway. We now get around town on bikes much more while trips into London or other cities are done by train.'

Streetcar, one of the fastest-growing of the car clubs, has vehicles parked a five-minute walk from Annabel's home. She uses the club for out-of-town journeys at weekends to visit family in Gloucestershire or short trips to the rubbish dump.

'We are about £2,500 a year better off by ditching the car and saving on petrol, vehicle maintenance and insurance,' she says. 'We now budget roughly £1,000 a year for using the car club.'

Due to demand for the service, Annabel has to plan at least a day in advance to guarantee a car when she wants to use it.

Streetcar, like competitors City Car Club and Zipcar, enables users to log on via a computer or a mobile phone to book vehicles, which are left in designated spaces that may be on the street or on accessible private property.

Certain phones, such as the iPhone, can operate as electronic keys to open the car. Otherwise members use magnetic swipe cards. Once inside, drivers enter a PIN into a dashboard device that releases the ignition key.

The cars are returned to the start point, although for an extra charge motorists may be able to leave them elsewhere.

The service is ideal for city dwellers or those who do not need a vehicle for routine journeys. As an added bonus for members in London, car club vehicles are exempt from the capital's congestion charge of £8 a day.

Car clubs work best for short hires, measured in hours. For longer-term rentals of a day or more, rates rise quickly and do not always compare favourably with rental firms.

Club cars tend to be cheaper to drive for the first few miles, but costs can climb where users exceed the free, allowable mileage, typically 30 miles a day.

Streetcar is the biggest car club, with more than 80,000 members and a fleet of 1,100 cars in eight cities. The annual membership costs £59.50.

Members get a smartcard key, fully comprehensive insurance and 24-hour breakdown support. Prices start at £4.95 an hour for a VW Polo, rising to £8.95 an hour for a BMW 3 Series or a VW Transporter.

For bookings under 72 hours, the cost of fuel is included for the first 30 miles a day with additional petrol charged at 23p a mile. The standard damage excess with Streetcar is £750, but this can be reduced to zero with an additional monthly fee of £14.95. The car can be dropped off at a different agreed destination from the pick-up point for a minimum £24.50 extra.

City Car Club has more than 20,000 members, who pay £50 a year with hourly charges from £4.95 for a Ford Fiesta to £7.95 for a VW Transporter. City Car Club has 550 vehicles in 14 cities.

Members are charged 19p a mile to cover the cost of fuel. Fully comprehensive insurance is included but there is a £500 excess – reduced to £100 if you pay an additional monthly £5.

The sector is consolidating as users see the benefits of joining a club with the biggest possible fleet. City Car Club took over rival WhizzGo in August last year. Streetcar, the biggest club in London, where car club usage is greatest, is seeking to merge with American rival Zipcar. However, the deal was referred to the Competition Commission and a decision is expected next January.

Zipcar charges £50 a year for membership, with rates from £3.95 an hour for a Honda Jazz to £6.95 for a BMW 3 Series. Fuel with Zipcar is free for the first 60 miles every day and 23p a mile after that.

⇨ This article first appeared in the *Daily Mail*, 2 October 2010.

DAILY MAIL

Road deaths fall to 2,222 in 2009

Latest road accident statistics.

Today the Department for Transport has published the new *Road Casualties Great Britain* report for 2009.

➪ There were a total of 222,146 reported casualties of all severities in 2009, 4% lower than in 2008;

➪ 2,222 people were killed, 12% lower than in 2008;

➪ 24,690 were seriously injured (down 5%); and

➪ 195,234 were slightly injured (down 4%).

The number of fatalities fell for almost all types of road user, with a fall of 16% for car occupants, 13% for pedestrians, 10% for pedal cyclists and 4% for motorcyclists.

Compared with the 1994–98 average, in 2009:

➪ The number killed was 38% lower;

➪ The number of reported killed or seriously injured casualties was 44% lower;

➪ The number of children killed or seriously injured was 61% lower; and

➪ The slight casualty rate was 37% lower.

In contrast, traffic rose by an estimated 15% over this period.

Edmund King, AA President, said:

'We hope that this all-time low in road deaths can be beaten next year but this will be a real challenge given the cuts to public expenditure which have already hit some road safety budgets and led to some local authorities switching off street lights. Questions have to be asked about the size of cuts that will fall on road maintenance, road safety schemes, road policing and road safety campaigns. If these cuts are made in the wrong places the progress made in recent years may not continue.

'As a society we should not accept that 2,222 should die on our roads. We must continue to invest in engineering, enforcement and education to make our roads safer. Drivers can help by pledging to always wear a seat-belt, never drink or drug drive, never use a mobile and by paying more attention. "Failed to look" was the most common contributory factor reported in 38% of crashes.'

Contributory factors

'Failed to look properly' was again the most frequently reported contributory factor and was reported in 38% of all accidents reported to the police in 2009.

Four of the five most frequently reported contributory factors involved driver or rider error or reaction.

For fatal accidents the most frequently reported contributory factor was loss of control, which was involved in 36% of fatal accidents.

Exceeding the speed limit was reported as a factor in 5% of accidents, but these accidents involved 17% of fatalities.

> *'Failed to look properly' was again the most frequently reported contributory factor and was reported in 38% of all [road] accidents reported to the police in 2009*

At least one of 'exceeding the speed limit' and 'travelling too fast for the conditions' was reported in 13% of all accidents and these accidents accounted for 27% of all fatalities.

'Pedestrian failed to look properly' was reported in 58% of accidents in which a pedestrian was injured or killed, and 'pedestrian careless, reckless or in a hurry' was reported in 23%.

23 September 2010

➪ The above information is reprinted with kind permission from the Automobile Association (AA). Visit www.theaa.com for more information.

© *Automobile Association (www.theaa.com)*

Transport and global poverty

Information from Practical Action.

One of the major causes of poverty is isolation. Improving the access and mobility of the isolated poor paves the way for access to markets, services and opportunities. By improving transport poorer people are able to access markets where they can buy or sell goods for income, and make better use of essential services such as health and education.

No proper roads or vehicles mean women and children are forced to spend many hours each day attending to their most basic needs, such as collecting water and firewood. This valuable time could be used to tend crops, care for the family, study or develop small business ideas to generate much-needed income.

Governments in developing countries recognise that a greater choice of transport is good for the population, but priority is usually given to building main roads that only serve the better-off. People in the poorest rural communities rarely benefit.

For more than 40 years, Practical Action have worked with poor communities to identify the types of transport that work best for them. With our technical and practical support, isolated rural communities can design, build and maintain village roads and bridges using local materials, tools and labour.

All Practical Action's projects are developed with the active participation of local people so they are right for their culture, needs and skills, and develop solutions that are sustainable.

Driving forward new ideas

Practical Action and the communities we work with are constantly crafting and honing new ideas to help poor people.

Recent developments include:

⇨ new equipment and training to make affordable, durable wheels and brakes;

⇨ bicycles that can carry bigger loads;

⇨ ropeways to transport farm produce across hillsides and rivers to local markets;

⇨ boats to transport people and goods in areas prone to flash flooding.

These practical, effective and easy-to-use forms of transport can prove life-changing. Aizul Pradesh, who runs his own boat service in Bangladesh, is proud of what he has achieved through his work with Practical Action. He says, 'During severe flooding I can now save families from my community by taking them to higher ground.'

Breaking the cycle of poverty

The wheel revolutionised the history of the world – and it continues to transform people's lives today. Practical Action makes a real impact on poverty by helping local communities develop different kinds of cycle-based transport. Bicycle ambulances, for instance, have helped save lives in Sri Lanka, Sudan, Nepal and Kenya. Quick and efficient, they provide a way of getting sick people to clinics and hospitals.

Cycle trailers have a practical business use too, helping people carry their goods, such as vegetables and charcoal, to markets for sale. Not only that, but those on the poverty-line can earn a decent income by making, maintaining and operating bicycle taxis.

With Practical Action's know-how, Sri Lankan communities have been able to start a bus service and maintain the roads along which it travels. The impact has been remarkable. This service has put an end to rural people's social isolation. Quick and affordable, it gives them a reliable way to travel to the nearest town; and now their children can get an education, making it far more likely they'll find a path out of poverty.

Bringing people on board

Working with local communities, Practical Action lobbied for government policies that would give poor people better, more affordable transport options to improve lives. In Kenya and Sri Lanka we have worked with town planners to ensure that the needs of cyclists were considered, vehicle pollution was reduced and good transport was available to even the poorest people.

Furthermore, in Kenya we have helped local communities influence the government to abolish bicycle import tax, while in Sri Lanka, lobbying from poor people encouraged the government and other donors to invest money in roads built by the local community.

As a founder member of the International Forum on Rural Transport and Development (IFRTD), Practical Action is at the heart of a global network that shares life-changing information about transport among individuals and organisations in nearly 100 countries. They are one of the leading publishers of technical manuals on low-cost vehicle manufacture and repair. They also provide information on village road construction and maintenance. Such practical advice helps rural people transform their lives.

⇨ Information from Practical Action. Visit www. practicalaction.org for more.

© Practical Action

PRACTICAL ACTION

Transport and the energy crisis

Transport accounts for around a third of all final energy consumption in the EEA member countries and for more than a fifth of greenhouse gas emissions.

I t is also responsible for a large share of urban air pollution as well as noise nuisance. Furthermore, transport has a serious impact on the landscape because it divides natural areas into small patches with serious consequences for animals and plants.

At the same time, transport is an essential element of our modern society: it ensures access to jobs, goods and services, education, leisure and tourism activities. Modern two-income households are even more dependent on transport because it is increasingly common that at least one person must commute a significant distance. This is partly a result of the increasing specialisation of labour. Furthermore, tasks such as shopping increasingly rely on transport because of the tendency for shopping areas to be concentrated in fewer places, away from residential areas, which are often devoid of shopping facilities.

Transport volumes are growing: 1.9% annually for passenger and 2.7% for freight transport. This growth is outpacing the improvements in energy efficiency of the various transport modes. As a result, energy consumption and emissions of greenhouse gases by transport are increasing. This is further exacerbated by a shift away from more environmentally efficient rail and bus transport towards cars and aircraft.

Transport is an essential element of our modern society: it ensures access to jobs, goods and services, education, leisure and tourism activities

A particular concern is aviation, which is the fastest-growing transport sector. This growth is partly driven by increasing wealth and low prices (aviation does not pay fuel tax), which underpin strong growth in tourism travel. Aviation now accounts for more than 10% of greenhouse gas emissions, if international aviation is included in the statistics.

In spite of the growth in transport, related emissions of harmful substances such as carbon monoxide, unburned hydrocarbons, particulates and nitrous oxides are decreasing as stricter emission standards are imposed for cars and trucks. Concentrations of particulate matter (PM) and ozone have, however, not generally shown any improvement since 1997. Fine particulate matter and ground-level ozone are now generally recognised as being the main threats to human health from air pollution, and transport is a main contributor to these.

One of the reasons why some air quality problems persist even though vehicles become cleaner, is that emissions in real driving conditions tend to be higher than emissions under test conditions.

Traffic noise affects a large share of the population. The World Health Organization estimates that about

40% of the population in the EU is exposed to road traffic noise at levels exceeding 55 dB(A), and that more than 30% is exposed to levels exceeding 55 dB(A) during the night.

Transport policies

Transport is integral to most activities in our society. It is therefore being dealt with by policy at all levels, from the global level (i.e. United Nations) to city councils. Of key importance is solving the dilemma between growth-oriented policies which tend to generate more transport, and environmental policies that call for emission reductions. The latter can be hard to achieve as long as technology improvements reducing emissions are outweighed by increasing transport volumes.

Global level

⇨ Emission standards for ships and aviation are dealt with by the respective UN organisations (International Maritime Organization and International Civil Aviation Organization) and by international conventions including the Convention on Long-range Transboundary Air Pollution which also addresses other sectors in addition to transport.

⇨ The Kyoto Protocol, part of the international Framework Convention on Climate Change, regulates greenhouse gas emissions including emissions from transport (except international aviation and maritime transport).

At the EU level

⇨ The guiding document is the EU common transport policy (2001, reviewed in 2006). This sets out the priorities for action on transport issues, including environmental aspects.

⇨ In addition, environmental policies and legislation deal with monitoring, emission reduction and air quality improvement (e.g. Environmental Noise Directive, National Emission Ceilings Directive, Cleaner Air for Europe Directive, vehicle emission limits and fuel quality).

National, regional and local levels

⇨ National transport policies deal partly with the transposition of EU policies into national legislation and partly with the development of the transport sector in each country.

⇨ The regional and local levels play an important role in practical land-use decisions which again have an important impact on transport demand as well as on the choice between transport modes faced by individual users. If new housing developments are not provided with access to public transport, people are left without a realistic choice.

⇨ The above information is reprinted with kind permission from the European Environment Agency. Visit www.eea.europa.eu for more information.

© European Environment Agency

Car travel

What can drivers do to reduce emissions?

⇨ For local travel consider leaving the car at home and either walk, cycle or use public transport.

⇨ Keep the vehicle properly serviced.

⇨ Check tyre pressures at least once a fortnight.

⇨ Avoid carrying unnecessary weight in the boot.

⇨ Plan the journey, so you don't get lost and waste fuel.

⇨ Try to avoid congested areas.

⇨ When starting up, there is no need to allow the engine to warm up – it is better to just drive off.

⇨ Try to avoid sudden acceleration, engine revving and sudden braking – harsh accelerating and braking can use up to 30% more fuel and increase wear and tear of the vehicle.

⇨ Avoid using air conditioning if possible, as this uses more fuel.

⇨ Drive with the windows closed, as this reduces drag on the vehicle.

⇨ Accelerate more slowly.

⇨ Switch the engine off if you think you are likely to be stationary for more than two minutes.

⇨ On motorways be aware of the three or four cars ahead, and keep a good distance from the car in front to avoid unnecessary braking.

⇨ When replacing your car, look for the most carbon efficient (i.e. with a low gCO_2/km figure) or with a high mpg – check out a car emissions calculator to see how much you could save.

⇨ The above information is reprinted with kind permission from carbonfootprint.com. Visit www.carbonfootprint.com for more information on this and other related topics.

© carbonfootprint.com

EUROPEAN ENVIRONMENT AGENCY / CARBONFOOTPRINT.COM

How heavy traffic harms us

Personal stories from the Campaign for Better Transport.

Cyclists

'I am a cyclist, and breathe in car exhaust fumes while cycling, have to take evasive action to avoid careless drivers, but can also see the detrimental effects of excessive car use on "communities": which are cut up, local shops are displaced to (car necessary) shopping centres on the outskirts of towns, and all the time increasing numbers of cars leads to increasing fear on the part of parents to let their children walk, let alone cycle, to school.'

Robin

'Cycling between the hours of 4pm and 6pm is very difficult in my area (Bury, Lancashire) because of very intimidating traffic. There is no way I would regularly commute by bike, particularly when the evenings are dark in winter. Therefore I commute by car, which adds to the general congestion.'

Martin

'I commute daily by bicycle, a round trip of some seven miles, perfect for cycling. I have been doing this for many years, although I also drive regularly, and I walk frequently. So I regard myself as a regular guy: I like to think I can see all sides of an issue. However, I do feel that heavy traffic is blighting our country more than ever. I believe the biggest deterrent to increased walking and cycling in this country is heavy road traffic. I would like to see more rights for walkers and cyclists and less for drivers. I would also like to see vastly more resources allocated to non-motorised transport, preferably by re-allocating resources away from road transport. Heavy traffic causes noise pollution which wrecks what could otherwise be calm, peaceful neighbourhoods. I could go on, and on, and on. My dad, a keen cyclist, always said he had been born at the start of the car boom and he hoped to live to see the end of it. I don't think he will quite make that, but I'm certainly hoping that I and my children will do.'

Paul

Public transport users

'Train prices are completely out of control and bear no relation to the service you get. I regularly travel by train, but in the last few years I have been regularly forced into other modes of transport due to the extreme cost of train travel. For example, I do Cardiff to Newcastle about four times per year to visit family. The normal quoted train price is about £120 return and takes about five hours. I can easily find flights for this amount, and often as little as £68 return. How on earth this can be at all logical in any Government's eyes is beyond me. Another example: I recently went to Edale in the Peak District from Cardiff. I was quoted a whopping £84 to take the train. I eventually decided to hire a car, which cost me £45 plus £30 petrol. If there had been two of us, the difference would have been off the scale. My problem is that I WANT to travel by train. I think it is efficient, environmentally sustainable and a much more pleasant way to travel. I really feel that people should not be so dependent on cars and short-haul flights, which pollute and consume more and more land for infrastructure... but I am being forced ONTO the roads.'

Adam

'I don't own a car and I rely on public transport. During the holidays I travel home from university by train (though it is cheaper by air). Even when I book in advance it is horribly expensive. I live in Wales and go to uni in Scotland. During reading week I can't afford to go home and I won't be able to get back home for the inter-semester break after exams either. I will have to take a chunk out of my overdraft to get home for Christmas. I don't own a car on principle, but when I talk to friends who do, they say that they couldn't live without them thanks to the state of public transport. How can we discourage people from using cars if they believe there is no alternative?'

Saoirse

⇨ The above information is reprinted with kind permission from the Campaign for Better Transport. Visit www.bettertransport.org.uk for more information on this and other related topics.

© Campaign for Better Transport

CAMPAIGN FOR BETTER TRANSPORT

The Congestion Charge

If you're planning to drive in central or west London it pays to find out how the Congestion Charge works or you might end up paying a hefty fine.

By Louis Pattison

The London Congestion Charge was far from universally popular when it passed into law in 2003, but despite early opposition from the Conservative Party – and even some London councils – it looks like it's here to stay.

Introduced to reduce traffic congestion in central London and raise investment to make much-needed repairs and upgrades to the city's transport system, the scheme has been largely hailed as a success. It's been reported that traffic levels in the zone have dropped by around 20%, cutting air pollution, clearing routes for buses and the emergency services, and making the roads safer for London's growing population of cyclists. Now, other large cities around the world are looking at London as a blueprint for introducing their own congestion zones.

It's been reported that traffic levels in the Congestion Charge zone have dropped by around 20%

How does the Congestion Charge work?

The Congestion Charge is a daily charge of £8 on motorists driving inside the Congestion Charge zone between 7am and 6pm, Monday to Friday. Don't expect to see toll booths or barriers, though. To pay, you register for an account at a shop or on the Transport for London (TfL) website.

The Congestion Charge is primarily there to reduce traffic at the capital's busiest times, so it gets days off like everyone else – you don't have to pay up on weekends, English public holidays or charging days that fall between Christmas Day and New Year's Day.

Where is the Congestion Charge zone?

The Congestion Charge zone currently covers a good chunk of central London, reaching down to Vauxhall Bridge in the south and up to Kings Cross in the north. (Look out for signs and a white-on-red C painted on the road.)

But while there were originally plans to roll the scheme out further into the suburbs, London Mayor Boris Johnson has ruled out any further growth, and there has been some speculation that he will dismantle the toll's western extension (introduced 2007). This would narrow the zone down to cover an area roughly between Buckingham Palace in the west and Tower Bridge in the east.

For drivers looking to cross London, there are also some free through routes – primarily, the route between Vauxhall Bridge Road and Edgware Road, and the Westway, which runs between Paddington and North Kensington. Visit the TfL website (www.tfl.gov.uk) for a map that shows the boundaries of the zone and all through routes.

Who is exempt from the charge – and can I get a discount?

Certain vehicles, including buses, taxis, ambulances, fire engines, motorcycles, some minibuses, small three-wheelers and vehicles that run on alternative fuel are exempt from the charge – although for many of these exemptions, you will still have to register to avoid receiving a fine.

If you live in or near the Congestion Charge zone you may be eligible for a 90% discount if you plan to pay the charge for a week or more at once. If you've been paying the Congestion Charge while waiting for your application to clear you may even be able to claim a refund on charges since applying.

If I don't pay, how will they catch me?

The system operates using a piece of surveillance technology called Automatic Number Plate Recognition. Cameras scattered around the zone read your number plate and check it off against a database to determine if you've paid or if you're exempt or have a discount. Failure to pay results in a fine of £120, which is reduced to £60 if paid within 14 days, but increases to £180 if unpaid after 28 days.

I've received a Penalty Charge Notice unfairly – how do I complain?

If you've simply forgotten to register, good luck, but that one probably won't wash. However, if you've received a Penalty Charge Notice (PCN) unfairly, you can make

a challenge to TfL. There have been reports that some motorists have been cloning number plates, resulting in innocent vehicle owners receiving penalty notices when their vehicles haven't been anywhere near the zone. It's up to you to prove your case, though. And before you get any ideas, be warned – displaying false plates can earn you fines of up to £1000, and the DVLA has the power to revoke their registration number, so best not to go there.

⇨ The above information is reprinted with kind permission from TheSite.org

Cyclists and motorists do not want to share road, report finds

Attempts to make cyclists and motorists share the road are doomed to failure, Government research has found.

By David Millward

While road users on two and four wheels live happily side by side in countries like Holland, the same is not true in Britain, according to the Department for Transport.

'The evidence suggests a failure in the culture of road sharing, with a lack of consensus about whether, and how, cyclists belong on our roads,' the report concludes. Cyclists who also drove displayed greater empathy towards motorists, the study found. The same applied towards drivers who occasionally took to two wheels.

But otherwise cyclists and motorists regarded each other with varying degrees of hostility.

According to the research cyclists could be divided into four categories.

There are those who do everything they can to avoid cars. This entails using only quiet streets and keeping as close to the kerb as possible.

Those who are slightly more confident will use some main roads, but keep as close to the left as they can. More assertive cyclists will cycle in the middle of the lane, but signal clearly to cars.

Then there are the opportunists who dodge and weave through traffic, recklessly cycling on the pavement and ploughing through red lights.

It was this final group which created what researchers found to be the stereotype of a cyclist: 'a kind of lawless freerider in the highly constrained and heavily taxed world of the driver.'

At the same time the study also found that motorists were impatient with cyclists, especially when they were feeling stressed for other reasons.

Some drivers were found to bitterly resent the very presence of cyclists on the road at all.

Mike Cavenett, spokesman for the London Cycling Campaign, said the only real solution was some form of segregation.

'When there are high volumes of traffic, driving at high speed, it has to be separated from cyclists.

'The only way we will get the sort of numbers of cyclists you see in Holland, with grandmothers and families on bikes, is when there is a sensation of safety.'

'Both cyclists and motorists have an equal right to use the roads'

Philip Gomm of the RAC Foundation voiced regret at the mutual antipathy. 'Some rivalries are enduring. Man U fans hate Man City fans. Labour supporters can't stand Tories. And it seems many car drivers continue to loathe cyclists, and vice versa.

'This is a shame because we share the same tarmac and we should be united in fighting for a better deal for all road users rather than having a pop at each other.'

Robert Gifford, Executive Director of the Parliamentary Advisory Council for Transport Safety, said: 'This research clearly poses a challenge. No single group of road users is entirely self-contained. During any one week, we will all be pedestrians; most of us will drive a car; some of us will make a journey by bike.

'We therefore need to develop a more inclusive approach to our fellow road users, seeing ourselves in their shoes as well as our own.'

A Department for Transport spokesman added: 'Both cyclists and motorists have an equal right to use the roads and it is vital for the safety of everyone that they are considerate to each other and obey the rules of the road.'

20 September 2010

Get moving!

What can you do about your transport carbon footprint?

Did you know?

⇨ Almost one third of students in the UK say they'd prefer to cycle to school or college but only 1% actually do!

⇨ The number of students getting a lift to school doubled in the last 20 years.

⇨ In a traffic jam, the pollution inside a car can be up to three times higher than outside.

Carbon footprint: transport

Cars account for a whopping 13% of the UK's CO_2 emissions. That's a massive contribution to global warming. More and more school runs are done by car even though there are other (greener) ways. And it's not just students either, teachers are just as bad. Transport is 17% of the carbon footprint of your average school or college. You could make a serious dent in this by getting staff and students out of cars and into the alternatives: cycling, walking and public transport. Not only are they much greener but they are healthier, cheaper, quicker (usually) and they give you more freedom. Read on for loads of practical ideas for projects to reduce your school or college's transport footprint.

CAR-FREE CHALLENGE Do Your Bit !

Tuesday 10th May

Set up a transport action group

First, get a good team who will take on the challenge of reducing the transport carbon footprint of your school or college. You need a good mix of students, teachers and non-teaching staff such as the caretaker/estates manager. Aim to meet at least once a term to plan activities and measure the impact. Need help setting up an action group? Check out our website: www. peopleandplanet.org/sixthforms/startagroup

Cars account for a whopping 13% of the UK's CO_2 emissions. That's a massive contribution to global warming

Counting the cars transport survey

You're probably thinking 'transport survey: boring!' But finding out how people travel now and what would make them switch to greener transport will be really useful to help you choose what to focus on. A painless way to do this is a hands-up survey – go round different classes/ tutor groups asking, how many people travel by car? Who would cycle or walk if there were better bike racks, cycle lessons or rewards like a free breakfast?

Organise a Car-Free Day

Plan! To make the day a success you need to plan. Hold a meeting to brainstorm your ideas for getting people out of their cars. Drag a staff member or two along to help you plan and get permission from the right people.

Maximise Your Impact! Hold your Car-Free Day during national Go Green Week in February, when People & Planet groups at schools, colleges and unis across the UK will all be taking action together. www. peopleandplanet.org/gogreenweek

Publicise! Make sure everyone in your school or college knows what's happening and how to get involved. Try:

⇨ assemblies on green transport;

⇨ stalls to sign people up to the 'car-free challenge';

⇨ notes in the register, emails and noticeboards (get staff on board to help with this);

⇨ put up eye-catching posters everywhere;

⇨ t-shirts, banners, green face paints...get creative!

PEOPLE AND PLANET

⇨ Use Car-Free pledge forms to gather support (available online).

Go for it!

Fill the day with fun activities like:

⇨ a competition between year/ tutor groups. Students earn points for leaving cars at home: get exciting prizes for the winners from the local council or cycle shops;

⇨ a 'buddies' scheme of older students walking with younger students;

⇨ a free breakfast for people who don't come by car;

⇨ get the Bike Doctor in to service people's bikes for free: http://bit.ly/CTgcT

⇨ cycling lessons from Bikeability: http://bit.ly/OSRWi

⇨ a fun gimmick like a bike-powered smoothie maker or sound system (your office contact can help sort this);

⇨ a car-sharing scheme.

Go Car-Free for good

It's no good having an amazing Car-Free Day if everyone instantly jumps back in the car once its over. You can keep people motivated by letting them know what a great thing they have done for themselves and the planet. Put up posters, write a story for the school/ college newsletter or P&P website and/or organise a prize-giving for the winning class/tutor group. Meet with the Head or Principal to make the case for a Car-Free Day or Week each year. It's not as scary as it sounds, heads and principals are really encouraged by student involvement and there's lots more info on how to arrange and prepare for this meeting on the website: www.peopleandplanet.org/gogreen/skills

Go green travel plan

Once you have a regular Car-Free Day, it's time to complete the transport revolution. By 2010 every school and college in the UK must have a plan to reduce car journeys. Make sure yours pushes for really ambitious aims and targets. What would your dream green travel school or college look like?

You might want to:

⇨ increase the number of pupils using green transport by 20% by 2012;

⇨ have a weekly Car-Free Day;

⇨ increase bike storage;

⇨ improve safety for walkers by providing more crossing points;

⇨ offer free training for all cyclists.

Present your ideas to the Head or Principal. There are lots of good arguments you could use, for example:

⇨ reduced congestion;

⇨ improved health, fitness and concentration of students;

⇨ can lead to funding for initiatives to promote active travel.

Ask your Head or Principal to read this Sustrans guide for more ideas: http://bit.ly/6O1tu

⇨ The above information is reprinted with kind permission from People and Planet. Visit www.peopleandplanet.org for more information on this and other related topics.

© People and Planet

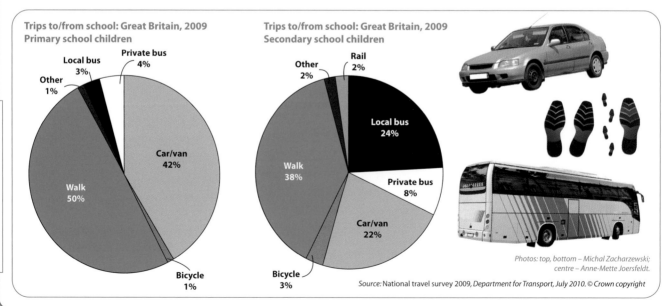

Trips to/from school: Great Britain, 2009
Primary school children

- Private bus 4%
- Local bus 3%
- Other 1%
- Car/van 42%
- Walk 50%
- Bicycle 1%

Trips to/from school: Great Britain, 2009
Secondary school children

- Rail 2%
- Other 2%
- Local bus 24%
- Private bus 8%
- Walk 38%
- Car/van 22%
- Bicycle 3%

Photos: top, bottom – Michal Zacharzewski; centre – Anne-Mette Joersfeldt.

Source: National travel survey 2009, Department for Transport, July 2010. © Crown copyright

PEOPLE AND PLANET

Travelling by bike

Cheap, reliable, green and keeps you fit. Is there any reason why you shouldn't be getting on your bike?

By Amy Turner

Travelling by bike is cheap – you don't have to buy a ticket to jump on a bike, and it won't need to be topped up with petrol. It's also reliable – no more waiting for buses that don't show up – and fast, with dedicated cycle lanes often letting you skip the traffic. It helps keep you fit and, with zero carbon emissions, it's good for the environment too.

Planning your route

Cycling on busy roads can be dangerous, so it's safer and more pleasant to make use of routes that aren't full of other traffic. Off-road, cyclists can ride on bridleways but public footpaths are off-limits.

The National Cycle Network, coordinated by the sustainable transport charity Sustrans, covers over 12,000 miles of traffic-free paths, quiet lanes and traffic-calmed roads. A map of the whole network can be downloaded from the Sustrans website and the site also has an interactive mapping facility that lets you find dedicated cycle routes near where you live.

Several local councils have produced their own cycling and walking maps showing recommended routes. Check with your local council to find out if there's one for your area.

Bike safety

Wherever you're cycling, wearing a helmet will help protect your head in the event of an accident. When choosing your helmet, it's vital you try it on before you buy. Helmets that don't fit snugly around your head will offer little or no protection, and you'll be put off wearing one that's uncomfortable.

It's also a good idea to wear light clothing or, ideally, high-visibility gear like a reflective vest. These help other road users to see you.

The rules of the road

As well as staying safe yourself, it's important to ride in a way that's safe for others. You should always give way to pedestrians and horse-riders, and use a bell to let them know you're coming.

If you cycle on the roads, the Highway Code applies as much to you as other drivers, so it's worth being aware of what rules apply to cyclists.

If you're cycling on the roads at night or in poor visibility, it's a legal requirement for your bike to have:

➩ a white front light;

➩ a red rear light;

➩ a red rear reflector;

➩ amber pedal reflectors on the front and rear of each pedal.

You are allowed to use either steady or flashing lights, provided they're bright enough.

Bike security

Whenever you leave your bike, it's important to lock it to something solid and immovable (ideally a proper cycle parking stand), in a well-lit area, using a strong lock. Solid D-locks are usually the most effective. It's worth putting a lock around the wheels as well as the frame, especially if they're quick-release.

It's a good idea to take a photograph of your bike and make a note of the frame number and any other distinguishing features. This information should help the police identify it if it ever gets stolen. It's also worth registering your bike for free with Immobilise and getting it property-marked or tagged.

You might also want to consider insuring your bike. If you live in a house that has contents insurance, the cheapest way to insure your bike is often through extending the existing policy. Otherwise, there are a number of companies out there that offer specialist insurance for bikes.

Taking your bike on public transport

If you're travelling a longer distance, you may want to take your bike with you on public transport. Most train companies allow bikes but you often have to book in advance, so check with the individual company before you travel. Local bus services don't usually allow bikes, but long-distance bus and coach services will often let you put a bike in the luggage hold if there's room. Again, check with the individual company. Folding bikes are much easier to carry on all forms of public transport and are usually treated as an ordinary piece of luggage.

➩ The above information is reprinted with kind permission from TheSite.org. Visit www.thesite.org for more information.

© TheSite.org

Is Europe's transport getting greener? Partly

While technological advances produce cleaner vehicles, more and more passengers and goods are travelling further distances, thereby offsetting efficiency gains.

Based on analysis of long-term trends, a new European Environment Agency (EEA) report calls for a clear vision defining Europe's transport system by 2050 and consistent policies to achieve it.

On its tenth anniversary, the EEA's TERM report presents an overview of transport's impact on the environment, built on an analysis of 40 policy-relevant indicators. The report's findings for the period 1997–2007 present a mixed picture, with some improvements in air pollutants and serious concerns regarding persistent growth in transport's greenhouse gas emissions.

'Over the last ten years we have concentrated on measures to improve mobility whilst decoupling transport emissions from economic growth. Today, we can see that the extensive investment in transport infrastructure has enabled us to travel further to meet our daily needs, but has not led to a decrease in the amount of time that we are exposed to noise, congestion and air pollution,' said Professor Jacqueline McGlade, Executive Director of EEA. 'In the future we will need to focus not only on the mode of transport, but also the reasons why people choose to travel, because ultimately mobility is inextricably linked to our quality of life.'

Transport, including international aviation and maritime transport, accounts for around a quarter of total EU greenhouse gas emissions. Unlike some sectors, transport's impact on the environment continues to be closely linked to economic growth.

Trends and findings

⇨ Freight transport tends to grow slightly faster than the economy, with road and air freight recording the largest increases in the EU-27 (43% and 35%, respectively, between 1997 and 2007). The share of rail and inland waterways in the total freight volumes declined during that period.

⇨ The current economic slowdown has reduced transport volumes but transport is expected to resume its growth as soon as the economy starts to grow again.

⇨ Passenger transport continued to grow but at a slower rate than the economy. Air travel within the EU remained the fastest growth area, increasing 48% between 1997 and 2007. Car journeys remained the dominant mode of transport, accounting for 72% of all passenger kilometres in the EU-27.

⇨ In EEA countries, greenhouse gas emissions from transport (excluding international aviation and maritime transport) grew by 28% between 1990 and 2007, and now account for around 19% of total emissions.

⇨ Despite recent reductions in air pollutant emissions, road transport was the largest emitter of nitrogen oxides and the second largest contributor of pollutants forming particulate matter in 2007.

⇨ Among 32 EEA countries, only Germany and Sweden are on track to meet their 2010 indicative targets for biofuels use.

⇨ Road traffic remains by far the largest source of exposure to transport noise. The number of people exposed to damaging noise levels, especially at night, is expected to increase unless effective noise policies are developed and implemented in full.

Background on the report

The EEA report *Towards a resource-efficient transport system* is the annual publication for the EEA Transport and Environment Reporting Mechanism (TERM), which monitors the progress and effectiveness of efforts to integrate transport and environment strategies.

TERM reports have been published since 2000 and offer important insights that can help the development of EU policies. The report aims to cover all EEA member countries.

About the European Environment Agency

The EEA is based in Copenhagen. The Agency aims to help achieve significant and measurable improvement in Europe's environment by providing timely, targeted, relevant and reliable information to policymakers and the public.

EEA member countries: Austria, Belgium, Bulgaria, Cyprus, the Czech Republic, Denmark, Estonia, Finland, France, Germany, Greece, Hungary, Iceland, Ireland, Italy, Latvia, Liechtenstein, Lithuania, Luxemburg, Malta, the Netherlands, Norway, Poland, Portugal, Romania, Slovak Republic, Slovenia, Spain, Sweden, Switzerland, Turkey, the United Kingdom.

⇨ Information from the European Environment Agency. Visit www.eea.europa.eu for more.

EUROPEAN ENVIRONMENT AGENCY

Investment in smarter travel means better health for all

Information from Sustrans.

With national debt high on the political agenda and the comprehensive spending review due in October [2010] isn't it time we began making wiser investment decisions?

Our public space is dominated by roads full of cars, causing pollution and creating a physical environment that discourages walking and cycling. This, in turn, contributes to a variety of health conditions including obesity, diabetes, coronary heart disease, stroke, osteoporosis, some cancers and mental health problems.

Our health budgets are burdened by the impact of obesity, with the economic implications weighing in at a substantial £49.9 billion by 2050. Promoting physical activity is now a public health priority. According to Department of Health figures, getting the nation more active could save every Primary Care Trust (PCT) an average of £5 million a year.

According to government figures, car traffic has increased some 15% in the last ten years, with congestion estimated to cost some £10 billion per year in English urban areas

Should public money be spent on the treatment of sedentary lifestyle diseases? Or should investment in creating safe walking and cycling conditions to provide routes to everyday destinations that are more conducive to a healthy lifestyle be a spending priority?

Huge cuts in public spending, rising congestion costs and soaring health bills from obesity and associated diseases will overwhelm government priorities unless action is taken.

Investing in enabling people to travel more often by foot, bike and public transport isn't just an incredibly cost-effective solution to transport challenges. It will also contribute enormously to government efforts to tackle spiralling health budgets.

According to government figures, car traffic has increased some 15% in the last ten years, with congestion estimated to cost £10 billion per year in

English urban areas. Meanwhile, significant reductions in transport spending will place severe pressure on transport budgets.

Using government methodology to measure the economic benefit to health of cycling, Sustrans found that the total health benefit to cyclists who used the National Cycle Network in 2008 was worth £270 million.

The evidence is now undeniable that the costs of our current transport system are large and that smarter travel choices provide opportunities to tackle not only the huge challenge of ill health, but also climate change, congestion, energy security and liveability.

The expected growth in major diseases, including obesity, coronary heart disease, stroke and diabetes in the next few years – especially those linked to physical inactivity – are likely to have a huge impact on the NHS.

As scrutiny on public spending is intensified, shouldn't future investment focus on interventions that deliver high value for money and benefits across government?

Sustrans is calling on UK governments to invest in doubling the number of journeys under five miles made by foot, bike and public transport to four out of five by 2020.

14 July 2010

⇨ Information from Sustrans. Visit www.sustrans.org.uk for more.

© Sustrans 2010, www.sustrans.org.uk

Transport: the way to go

Information from Friends of the Earth.

In a jam

The past 50 years have seen a revolution in the way we travel. We're able to travel further and faster and do more. Millions of us today have more independence and mobility than ever before. That's partly because most households in the UK now own a car.

But cars are a mixed blessing. The way we travel is having a huge impact on us, our environment and the economy. Air pollution from traffic makes asthma worse for millions of children. Thousands of people are killed or seriously injured on the roads every year. Some of our best countryside and most important wildlife sites are threatened by road-building. Congestion costs the economy billions of pounds every year. And aeroplanes are causing noise and pollution nightmares for tens of thousands of people.

Perhaps the biggest problem of all is transport's contribution to climate change through carbon dioxide (CO_2) emissions. Climate change is the world's greatest environmental challenge. It will hit developing countries hardest and they will be least able to cope with the impact. But the UK will also be affected.

We've been heading down the wrong road for too long, building more roads in an attempt to crack our transport crisis, but it doesn't work. We need to find a different route. That's why Friends of the Earth wants to see a transport system based around people, not cars and roads.

Road to ruin

In the past 30 years, traffic on our roads has more than doubled. More of us have cars and we're using them more.

Climate-changing emissions from road transport are forecast to rise for years to come. Because of climate change, extreme and unpredictable weather, flooding, droughts and the spread of tropical diseases are already having a devastating impact around the world. Getting control of transport emissions will be essential if the UK Government is to make yearly reductions in carbon dioxide output.

Many main roads are very congested. But new and wider highways don't solve the problems for long – they actually encourage longer journeys and generate more traffic. New roads cost hundreds of millions of pounds, which could be better spent in other ways – such as on promoting cycling, walking and public transport use

through 'smarter travel choices' initiatives which are proven to cut car trips. A national programme is estimated to cost £2 billion – the same as the Highways Agency's two most expensive new road schemes.

It's not easy living in a car-dominated society if you don't have a car, particularly if shops and hospitals are not within walking or cycling distance. Bus services are inadequate in many rural areas. Over half of Britain's poorest households don't have access to a car, yet many of these households live in the areas with most traffic, most accidents and worst pollution.

Roads make a mess of our countryside and take their toll on wildlife: for example, up to 45,000 badgers are killed on Britain's roads every year.

> *The past 50 years have seen a revolution in the way we travel. Millions of us today have more independence and mobility than ever before*

Cars will be part of transport in the future but we need to use them less than we do now and make sure they're less polluting.

Plane crazy

Cheap flights may be tempting, and aeroplanes have enabled us to visit places our grandparents only dreamed of, but aviation also causes big environmental and social problems.

The UK Government wants a huge expansion of aviation and is supporting the building of new runways or terminals at many UK airports to make this happen. Passenger numbers could more than double by 2030. This growth is only possible because airlines don't pay any tax on the fuel they use and pay no VAT on many parts of their operations. This amounts to an effective subsidy from the UK taxpayer of more than £9 billion every year – that's more than £100 per person in the country.

Aviation fuel has become one of the fastest growing sources of climate-changing gases. It could account for more than a tenth of UK emissions by 2020. Growth on the scale the Government wants would make it very difficult to reach our long-term targets to reduce emissions of climate-changing gases.

Tens of thousands of people live under flight paths, in some cases with planes passing overhead every couple of minutes throughout the day. Flights can create sleeping problems for many. Exposure to aircraft noise

has been linked to high blood pressure and children's reading difficulties.

Cheap flights are hitting the UK tourism industry, with people now taking more weekends abroad.

Friends of the Earth is challenging the Government's push for more air travel and is supporting local communities opposing airport expansion.

Transports of delight

There is a route out of our transport crisis: we need less traffic on our roads and less growth in aviation.

Real choices

People need real choices so that they don't have to use their cars as much. This doesn't mean giving up cars – they will still be the sensible choice for some journeys. Providing real choices means improving public transport and making streets safer for cycling and walking.

Travel less

We have to make it easier to leave the car at home. This means making sure people can get to the places they want to go – such as shops and jobs – by public transport, by bike or on foot. New technologies can enable people to work at home instead of commuting.

Greener cars

If cars are going to continue to be part of the way we travel, we have to make sure they do less damage to the environment. Financial incentives to buy more fuel-efficient, less polluting cars, like hybrids and electric cars, will help cut emissions of climate-changing gases. But the electricity grid must be rapidly decarbonised too.

Fair tax for aviation

Aviation gets off lightly in tax terms. We want Air Passenger Duty to be replaced with a Per Plane Duty that will cover freight flights and encourage airlines to fly fuller planes.

The sorts of policies Friends of the Earth want could cut traffic by a quarter at peak times. What we're asking for is already being done in France, Germany and the Netherlands.

What you can do

It's not just up to the Government to sort out our transport crisis. We can all make a difference by thinking about how we travel, and making changes at home, at work, at school or in our neighbourhoods.

Share a car

Think about whether you could share a car on a regular trip – to work, a football match, to church or the shops. Is there someone who lives near you going too? Sharing a car means one less vehicle on the road and alternating which car you use means one of you can relax on the journey.

Leave your car at home for two days a week

Find out whether you can get to work without having to use your car. Contact TransportDirect for public transport information or the national cyclists' organisation CTC for details of cycle routes in your area. Rest your car for a couple of days every week.

There is a route out of our transport crisis: we need less traffic on our roads and less growth in aviation

---

Get on your bike

Rather than drive to a gym to get some exercise, why not walk more or get out the bike again? Cycling and walking keep you fit and help reduce the risk of heart disease – and you can be out in the open air.

Shop locally

Use local shops rather than going to a supermarket that you have to drive to. You'll cut down on congestion and also support local businesses.

Holiday travel

The next time you need a break, try going by train. Trains are much less polluting than aeroplanes and you'll be helping local economies. Taking the train to many destinations in Europe can be cheaper than flying.

Set up a walking bus

Many children don't want to be driven to school. Walking buses are a fun way of enabling them to walk to school with parental supervision. Talk to other parents living near you about setting up a walking bus. More information from Sustrans (www.sustrans.org.uk).

Cut down on business trips

Do you really need to travel to meet with colleagues? Could you use phone or video conferencing? If you do need to travel, go by train rather than by car or plane – it's often quicker and you'll be able to get some work done.

July 2010

⇨ The above information is reprinted with kind permission from Friends of the Earth. Visit www.foe.co.uk for more information.

© *Friends of the Earth*

Do governments dream of electric cars?

'We will mandate a national recharging network for electric and plug-in hybrid vehicles,' is the proud pronouncement in the recently released Programme for Government.

Why? The argument seems to go something like this. Personal car use in the UK accounts for 13% of CO_2 emissions, and is dependent on oil. We need an 80% cut in CO_2 by 2050, and have an energy crisis looming. Reducing car use is too hard. Electric cars may, one day, be powered using nuclear energy. So let's get investing.

The argument forgets that currently over three-quarters of the UK's electricity comes from fossil fuels, and electric cars will remain heavily dependent on coal, gas and oil for some years to come.

And in an energy-constrained world, what's the priority? Growing food, running hospitals, heating schools and homes, powering public transport – or an electric car fleet carrying 1.6 people a trip?

New vehicle technology gets taken up very slowly, with it usually taking ten to 20 years to achieve 5% of new sales

Let's not forget that electric cars will not address the impact of busy roads on the liveability of our communities, or the fear of speeding traffic which has seen the number of children playing outside their front door drop from 75% in the 70s to 15% today. It will not address our spiralling obesity epidemic in which sedentary travel is heavily implicated, or our 'obesogenic environment' created by public space dominated by traffic that makes walking or cycling unpleasant. We will go on spending, as we already do, many billions annually on dealing with the consequences of the UK's very high levels of car use.

New vehicle technology gets taken up very slowly, with it usually taking ten to 20 years to achieve 5% of new sales. Perhaps even more worryingly, most government scenarios even think it unlikely that electric vehicles will number more than 25% of new sales by 2050.

So what can be done now, and cheaply, to save us chasing a red herring?

Evidence shows that two out of five local journeys are already made by foot, bike and public transport. With the right investment the UK can increase this to four out of five local journeys.

Sustrans' work with households to change people's travel behaviour has reduced car use by up to 14% just by informing people where their local walking, cycling and bus routes go. Sustrans' work giving children cycling skills and confidence doubles the number of kids cycling daily to school, often clearing roads of cars on the school run.

And there is overwhelming evidence, from the Cycling Demonstration Towns to the Sustainable Travel Demonstration Towns, that money invested in enabling people to choose to leave their car behind is money well spent. Evidence that is somewhat lacking for electric cars.

"What's that on the side of the road Dad?"

"It's called a footpath son. Apparently people used to walk once!"

So there are already plenty of affordable and immediate options for de-carbonising and reducing the energy intensity of travel. And for longer journeys we've got low-carbon options called buses and trains.

So let's put the mandate into increasing levels of walking, cycling and public transport use. Our environment, health, wellbeing and communities will all be the winners, and we'll save a lot of money, energy and natural resources.

⇨ The above information is reprinted with kind permission from Sustrans. Visit www.sustrans.org.uk for more information.

© Sustrans 2010, www.sustrans.org.uk

SUSTRANS

UK electric car grant scheme 'cut by 80%'

Government commits to just £43m of the original £230m promised for programme to subsidise the uptake of electric cars.

By Adam Vaughan

A government grant scheme to give motorists up to £5,000 off the cost of a new electric car has been cut by 80%, opposition politicians and green campaigners claimed today. The fate of a network of charging points to power such low-emission cars also hangs in the balance.

Following lobbying from electric car-makers, who argued abolishing the incentive would harm the cars' take-up and hit the creation of green jobs, Transport Secretary Philip Hammond today confirmed the grant will go ahead in January 2011.

> **Under the 'plugged-in car grant' scheme, buyers of new electric cars will be offered up to 25% off the car's price, capped at a maximum of £5,000**

'The Coalition Government is absolutely committed to low-carbon growth, tackling climate change and making our energy supply more secure,' said Hammond. 'This will ensure that the UK is a world leader in low-emission vehicles.'

However, the Government has committed only to an initial fund of £43m, to run until March 2012, which will be reviewed in January 2012. Under the original £230m scheme first announced in March 2010 by Labour, there was no plan to review the scheme annually, said a spokesperson for Shadow Transport Secretary Sadiq Khan.

But a spokesperson for the Department for Transport (DfT) said the £43m in the first year was the same level of spending under the Coalition's plans as it was under the former administration's. The first tranche of money could fund up to 8,600 cars, assuming all buyers took full advantage of the £5,000 discount.

Under the 'plugged-in car grant' scheme, buyers of new electric cars will be offered up to 25% off the car's price, capped at a maximum of £5,000. All of the first generation of electric cars eligible for the grant, such as the Nissan Leaf, Mitsubishi i-MiEV and Telsa Roadster sports car, cost over £20,000.

Khan said: 'This announcement goes nowhere near matching the ambition of the scheme as set out by Labour – there is money here for less than a quarter of the new low-carbon vehicles we envisioned. Thanks in part to this scheme and a grant from the last government, Nissan chose to manufacture its low-carbon Leaf model in Sunderland. By making Britain one of the world's leading markets for low-carbon vehicles, we could attract more manufacturers here. But to make that happen the Coalition must show greater ambition than this.'

There is also still uncertainty over a related 'plugged-in places' project announced under the previous government to build thousands of new charging points to top up the vehicles on public streets. Almost all of the cars have a maximum range of 100 miles or less. The Government said today that a decision on the financing and number of such points would be delayed until the comprehensive spending review in the autumn.

> **'Electric cars are one of the ways we can cut our dependence on oil'**

Greenpeace transport campaigner Vicky Wyatt said: 'Electric cars are one of the ways we can cut our dependence on oil and move towards a clean, green transport system. That's why it's good news that the Government has announced this first chunk of funding. But if the Government is serious about putting hundreds of thousands more electric cars on Britain's roads, it's vital that Phillip Hammond makes a long-term commitment and stumps up the full £230m, as promised by the previous government.'

'Nissan welcomes today's announcement by the Government to offer consumer incentives for electric vehicles,' said a company spokesperson. 'In doing so, the Government has signalled that Britain is serious about supporting new low-carbon technologies and is serious about helping consumers to make more sustainable choices.'

Energy and Climate Change Secretary Chris Huhne said: 'Electric and low-carbon cars are fun to drive and essential to meet our climate targets. That's why we'll need a massive increase in the number of electric and clean green cars on our roads. Because this is new technology the Government needs to step in to kick-start the market, which is why today's initiative is vital.'

28 July 2010

© *Guardian News and Media Limited 2010*

THE GUARDIAN

Electric buses: green public transport or THE public transport?

Electric buses are not just good for the environment; they may actually be more suited to the role.

The increasing urgency for greener modes of public transport has seen the electric bus take centre stage as a potential solution, but could electric public transport be superior to conventional diesel engines even beyond their environmental benefits?

China moved closer to urban dependence on the electric bus in March 2009, with the introduction of a new fleet of Ankai electric buses to Shanghai. Although intended to lower air pollution levels, passengers have noted additional features of the buses that make them preferable to diesel alternatives – a common find in cities around the world. Electric public transport is beginning to prove itself as more than an environmental alternative to diesel vehicles; in fact, it may actually be more suited to the role the vehicle performs.

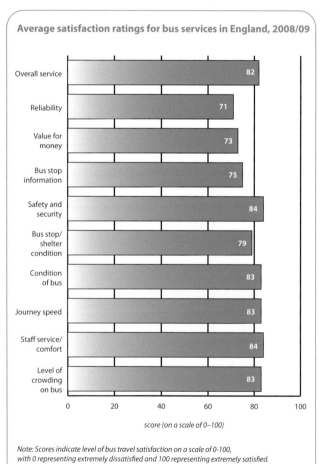

Average satisfaction ratings for bus services in England, 2008/09

	score
Overall service	82
Reliability	71
Value for money	73
Bus stop information	75
Safety and security	84
Bus stop/ shelter condition	79
Condition of bus	83
Journey speed	83
Staff service/ comfort	84
Level of crowding on bus	83

score (on a scale of 0–100)

Note: Scores indicate level of bus travel satisfaction on a scale of 0-100, with 0 representing extremely dissatisfied and 100 representing extremely satisfied.

Source: Public Transport Statistics Bulletin GB: 2009 Edition, Department for Transport/ONS, © Crown copyright

Electric bus advantages

The electric engine does not result in a bus that is simply more environmentally friendly yet of a lower quality: in fact, the overall performance is arguably improved. In addition to their main quality of a reduction in air pollution due to the lack of emissions, electric transport has proven itself adept at ascending steep hills en route, making the electric tram ever popular in San Francisco.

The electric engine causes far less vibration throughout the vehicle, making for a more comfortable journey for those on board without the 'rattling' often experienced when a bus is at lights or a stop. A reduction in vibration also increases the life and reduces maintenance requirements of the bus or tram, making it a cost-effective option for operators.

The increasing urgency for greener modes of public transport has seen the electric bus take centre stage as a potential solution, but could electric public transport be superior to conventional diesel engines even beyond their environmental benefits?

Although the initial introduction of an electric transport system and fleet can be costly, as a long-term mode of public transport trolley buses are surprisingly cost-effective in terms of lifespan and upkeep.

One of the most common causes of approval for the electric bus is its lack of noise. The electric buses are noticeably quiet, lowering noise pollution and increasing comfort for those on board.

Regenerative braking demonstrated with the electric bus means that the motor acts as a generator, channeling excess energy back into the battery and wires of the bus. Diesel buses would see this energy expelled as friction during braking, meaning that the electric bus saves around 30% of energy through this difference alone.

The necessary infrastructure associated with the presence of electric buses in a city contributes to their

eco-friendly image around the area and reinforces the notion that the system is viable as a permanent one. Arnhem in the Netherlands saw use of local buses increase by 17%, an encouraging reflection of general public support for convenient green transport alternatives.

Electric trams: disadvantages

A similar alternative to the bus would be the tram. However, one of the most obvious disadvantages of the modern tram is its confinement to a set route by the wires or tracks. In the case of a diversion en route, the tram is faced with limited alternative routes through an area, alarming in the case of a bomb or safety threat ahead. Additionally, a new tram route would have to involve heavy construction work and large-scale traffic disruption.

The future for electric buses

Hino, a division of Toyota, are currently testing wireless electric buses using electromagnetic inductive charging technology, the method used to charge objects such as the electric toothbrush. Inductive charging sees the embedding of induction coils into the surface of the road, which will reverberate power to the passing bus and can be stored in the vehicle's batteries. The main advantage of this ideology is that the electric bus will not be required to stop its operation in order to be recharged, yet it will be charged with far stronger power than if relying on a battery.

Alternative charging systems for electric buses would include rapid charging systems that could be installed at specific bus stops. The myth that an electric battery would not have a sufficient charge for the job is simply not true and would be no different from a current diesel bus having to use a filling station at the bus depot.

Inherent installation costs associated with this method of powering buses will need to be reduced and further justified so they can begin to replace traditional versions. The cost of purchasing a fleet of electric buses can also be very costly compared to a diesel fleet. However, as mentioned earlier, the running costs are far lower and now developers' sights are pointing in the right direction to evolve the electric bus still further for its role in the future.

23 June 2009

⇨ The above information is reprinted with kind permission from Enviro News and Business. Visit www.enviro-news.com for more information.

Giant bus which drives over cars planned in China

A giant bus which runs on wheeled 'legs' that allow cars to drive underneath it has been designed by a Chinese company.

By Tom Chivers

The huge vehicle is as wide as two road lanes and 18 feet tall, carries more than 300 passengers per bus, and its electric motors run partly on solar power. The bus network could carry as many as 1,400 passengers at once.

Building the buses and a 40km (25-mile) track for them would cost 500 million yuan (£46.5 million), about ten per cent the cost of the equivalent distance of underground railway

Its designers say it can reduce traffic congestion in China's crowded cities by as much as 30 per cent.

Furthermore, it is said that each bus can reduce fuel use by 860 tons per year, bringing carbon emissions down by 2,640 tons.

Song Youzhou, the chairman of Shenzhen Hashi Future Parking Equipment Company, the firm behind the buses, says: 'The main innovation of the straddling bus is that it runs above cars and under overpasses. Its biggest strengths are saving road space, efficiency and high capacity.'

The bus will need to have the roads it runs on redesigned – either with rails for the bus to run on, or simple white lines that an automated system can use as guides. The rails would be more expensive, but Mr Youzhou says they would make the buses a further 30 per cent more efficient. Building the buses and a 40km (25-mile) track for them would cost 500 million yuan (£46.5 million), about ten per cent the cost of the equivalent distance of underground railway.

In the event of emergencies, passengers would escape from the bus using an inflatable slide, like on passenger aircraft.

It is expected to be put into use in Beijing's Menougou District in the 'near future', although a specific time frame is not known.

Story via Discovery News.
6 August 2010

Developing city-scale sustainable transport networks

Better public transport, walking and cycling provision help reduce carbon emissions in cities.

Portland in the USA is a good example of an integrated transport system, with buses, light rail, streetcars, a free rail zone, an aerial tram and bicycle network.

Light rail has been developed in Manchester, Nottingham, the West Midlands, Tyne and Wear and Sheffield. Light rail development in many large towns and cities in France has demonstrated how high-profile infrastructure can help to regenerate cities and hugely improve image and liveability.

Further information on some of these international examples is available from the Light Rail Transit Association.

In London, examples of major planned city-wide public schemes include Crossrail, the Overground network which provides much needed orbital links, the Dockland Light Railway and the Tramlink. The London bus priority network is more advanced than most other cities in the UK. New forms of public transport are also being trialled in London, such as ultra-light rapid transit at Heathrow Airport.

Elsewhere, guided bus systems have been developed. There is a guided busway in Leeds and there are plans for a new system in Cambridge. More established schemes can be found in Ottawa (Canada), Brisbane (Australia), Nancy and Caen (France), Transmilenio (Colombia) and Curitiba (Brazil).

Using public space and green infrastructure to provide high-quality, safe environments for moving around cities and within and between neighbourhoods can encourage people to choose to walk and cycle more

Both light rail and guided bus systems provide effective city-wide opportunities. The choice between systems will need to be based on proper analysis, with discussion of the drivers and worked examples of the costs and benefits. The relative capacities of guided bus systems and light rail vary by specification, with light rail generally having a greater capacity (up to 30%). The capital costs of light rail are also usually higher than guided bus systems, but this is dependent on the extent and nature of the service.

A strategy for street design can be established to support public transport use and walking and cycling. This can be based on objectives reflecting a street's role as both a place and a way of getting about. A range of different options exists to change the allocation of space on the roads. Options include the development of greater pedestrian provision, bus and cycle lanes, shared spaces and routing strategies.

Bremen, Groningen and Bologna have developed innovative traffic management initiatives using 'traffic

cells', the borders of which cannot be crossed by private cars, only by public transport, on foot or by bicycle, thereby making non-local travel by car more difficult.

Copenhagen offers an example of a city-wide cycle network. An extensive cycle network is complemented by the provision of city cycles and convenient storage and repair centres for public use. A key aspect is the integration of cycles with public transport – suburban stations are typically 'cycle and ride'. Portland, USA aims to create a 'low stress bikeways network' where people of all ages and abilities feel happy to cycle around the city.

The Vélib' cycle programme in Paris – an abbreviation of 'vélo' (bike) and 'liberté' (freedom) – and similar schemes in Lyon, Seville, Vienna and elsewhere, are also very impressive. Cycles are provided for hire across the city at a nominal price. Cycle hire is available 24 hours a day, seven days a week. Thousands of bikes are available from multiple pick-up and drop-off locations. These allow the picking up of bikes at one location and dropping off at another. A similar scheme will start in London in summer 2010.

In the UK, Milton Keynes, Stevenage, Harlow and many of the UK New Towns have excellent cycle networks. Relatively low usage, however, highlights that infrastructure provision alone is insufficient to ensure high levels of cycling. Effective urban structure and a cycling culture are also required.

Peterborough's millennium green wheel is an 80km network of cycle paths and walking routes that encircle the city and are joined by 'spoke' routes through parks and along riversides joining the city to the surrounding countryside. Exeter has a 'Beauty and the Bike' programme, aimed at encouraging cycling for girls.

Using public space and green infrastructure to provide high-quality, safe environments for moving around cities and within and between neighbourhoods can encourage people to choose to walk and cycle more. Likewise, creating pleasant, safe public transport nodes will increase the attractiveness of using public transport. Cycle parking provision is also very important to support use of the wider network and encourage people to choose cycling for a commute to work, for example.

The entire approach to the structure of a city can be used to support the development of sustainable transport systems. Curitiba is a Brazilian city of 1.6 million people where 75 per cent of commuters use public transport. Traffic levels have declined by 30 per cent since 1974, even though the population has doubled. High-density development is permitted around express busway corridors and the allowable densities decline as distance increases from the express busway. Lower density areas are served by local feeder bus services.

The Curitiba bus system is a financially self-sufficient project that has been achieved through an integrated approach involving changes in the planning system, a diversified public transport service, variable concentration of residential development according to proximity to the transport network, the creation of dedicated road facilities, the introduction of innovative 'loading tubes', and the evolution of a special relationship between the public and private sectors. Local community groups were involved in the planning process.

⇨ The above information is reprinted with kind permission from CABE and Urban Practitioners. Visit www.cabe.org.uk or www.engagingplaces.org.uk for more.

© CABE/Urban Practitioners

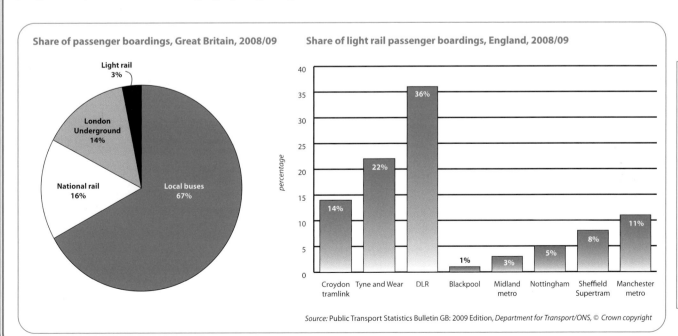

Share of passenger boardings, Great Britain, 2008/09

- Light rail 3%
- London Underground 14%
- National rail 16%
- Local buses 67%

Share of light rail passenger boardings, England, 2008/09

	percentage
Croydon tramlink	14%
Tyne and Wear	22%
DLR	36%
Blackpool	1%
Midland metro	3%
Nottingham	5%
Sheffield Supertram	8%
Manchester metro	11%

Source: Public Transport Statistics Bulletin GB: 2009 Edition, *Department for Transport/ONS,* © *Crown copyright*

CABE / URBAN PRACTITIONERS

Guided busways: frequently asked questions

Information from Britpave.

What is a guided busway?

A guided busway is usually a dedicated, buses-only route with buses running on a purpose-built track. The bus is guided along the route so that steering is automatically controlled and, like a tram, the vehicle follows a set path. The bus driver controls the speed of the vehicle.

How are guided buses guided?

Kerb-guided buses are normal, everyday buses with a driver at the wheel. What makes them different is small guide wheels attached to the front wheels of the bus, that run along the vertical face of kerbs on a purpose-built track called a guideway. The guide wheels steer the bus whilst it's in the guideway.

Guideways can be used for part or all of a bus route. Guided buses can be either low-speed operations, introduced to relieve congestion in busy towns, or high-speed operations, which provide 'light rapid transit' (LRT) over longer distances.

Other guided bus technology uses remote guidance by radio, electro-magnetic or optical systems, but Britpave, and its website, is concerned with kerb-guided bus systems, and the role of slip-forming in constructing the guideways.

What's the point of a guided bus?

Like a railway line, the guideway excludes all other traffic, giving the bus a clear road ahead, even in congested areas during rush hours. Therefore the service is fast and reliable: at peak periods, guided buses can arrive at frequent intervals.

All these factors mean guided buses can deliver a high standard of public transport akin to a metro, light rail or tram system. Unlike a train or tram, though, the bus can leave the busway at certain junctions and drive on normal roads, giving it the flexibility to provide on-road services too and allowing passengers get on or off close to their homes or at any key location in the area.

Why not use bus lanes or bus-only roads?

Bus lanes and bus-only roads are open to illegal use by other road users for queue jumping and parking. This abuse slows bus journeys and drains resources as breaches of bus lanes need to be monitored and fines have to be issued for misuse. With its kerbs and narrow width, a guided busway is not accessible by most vehicles, virtually eliminating the abuse of the bus route.

Guided busways can also be built in areas too narrow for standard bus lanes, including disused railway lines with embankments – land that could never be made into a road.

Why not use a light rail or a metro system?

Guided bus systems are less expensive than light rail or metro systems. Like light rail, a guided bus service can be high speed, reliable and comfortable. It also has the advantage of the transport not being fixed to the rail, with the bus being able to leave the guideway and drive down any road as does a standard bus, enabling bus stops to be located within the community.

Guided busways do not require the overhead electrification or signalling systems usually needed to operate light rail or metro systems.

Are there environmental benefits to a guided busway?

A guided busway has many environmental advantages over a traditional tarmac road. A guided busway can offer better drainage than a solid tarmac road, as water can drain away between the guideway tracks. The guideway also takes up less space than a standard road lane. The route can be landscaped and planted alongside and between the tracks, making the busway very green to the eye, absorbing engine noise and allowing the biodiversity of an area to exist alongside the transport system. Such landscaping also makes the busway look very different to a road, discouraging other road users from accidentally entering it.

Studies have shown that more people use the guided buses than use conventional buses in bus lanes or bus-only roads. This indicates that guided buses are more successful in encouraging car users to switch to public transport, another benefit for the environment.

To bring further benefits to the community, Britpave recommends building a maintenance strip/bridleway alongside a guideway to open up access for pedestrians, cyclists and horse riders. This also discourages trespass on the guideway as people have a clear and safe alternative to dangerously entering the guideway.

Finally, with many low-emission and now hybrid buses available, the bus itself can be seen as an increasingly green method of transport.

⇨ The above information is reprinted with kind permission from Britpave. Visit www.britpave-bus-rail.org.uk for more.

© Britpave

What is a tram?

What exactly is a tram? What is the difference between trams and light rail? What distinguishes trams and light rail from conventional railways?

Trams and light rail are forms of urban public transport; with a handful of exceptions, tramways and light rail systems across the world are almost exclusively passenger-carrying operations. There is no hard and fast definition of what constitutes 'light rail' or what the difference is between light rail and trams, and there are different opinions on what exactly the terms mean, but this article should give you an idea.

Trams

A tram, usually known in North America as a 'streetcar', 'trolleycar' or 'trolley', is a vehicle which runs on fixed rails and is designed to travel on streets, sharing road space with other traffic and pedestrians. Most tram systems also include at least some off-street running, either along the central reservation of roads (what would be called the 'median strip' in the US) or on fully segregated alignments. Such sections of a route can be called 'reserved rights of way'. Some tram systems run mostly on reserved tracks, with only short stretches of on-street running. Many of the tram systems in the UK utilise former railway alignments, or share what were previously railway-only alignments with heavy rail services.

TRAMS, THEY'RE ... – JUST PART OF THE CROWD!

The tracks that a tram runs on are called a tramway; the system itself can be called a tramway system.

First generation tramways

Horse-drawn tramways were first introduced at the beginning of the 19th century. The first electric tramway began operation in Germany in 1881, and existing horse-drawn tramways were progressively converted to electric operation. With the emergence of motorbuses and trolleybuses (also known as trackless trolleys) which run on rubber tyres without needing rails, tramways started to fall out of favour. In many countries (the UK and the US for example), many tram systems were abandoned in favour of these alternative forms of mass transit; the rising popularity of private cars also had a detrimental effect on the viability of tramways. In Britain, by the end of 1962 all but one tramway system (Blackpool) had closed. In North America, all but a tiny handful of tramways had closed by the mid-1960s. Many systems remained open in continental Europe, and have been progressively modernised.

> *Trams and light rail are forms of urban public transport; with a handful of exceptions, tramways and light rail systems across the world are almost exclusively passenger-carrying operations*

Light rail

The term 'light rail' is used to describe railway operations using smaller vehicles which have a lower capacity and lower speed than conventional railways; light rail infrastructure is designed to be cheaper to build and maintain. Light rail is an intermediate transport mode, catering for short intra- and inter-urban journeys – stops are generally closer together than commuter railways but further apart than local bus routes.

Because of the nature of the technology used, light rail systems are often subject to less stringent operational regulation than conventional railways, which leads to greater operational flexibility. For instance, 'heavy rail' systems will normally be required to operate block signalling systems which create an absolute limit on track capacity – maximum headway. By contrast many

light rail systems, by virtue of their slower speeds, lighter vehicle construction and shorter braking distances, are able to operate on line-of-sight, allowing vehicles to pull up right behind one another, meaning there is virtually no limit to track capacity.

Tram-train...features hybrid vehicles which travel into a city on main line railway tracks, under diesel power if necessary, before switching to tram tracks and electric power for the journey through the city centre

Light rail systems typically feature high-frequency services, removing the need for anything more than the most basic public timetables. Stops are often less substantial than conventional railway stations, and are generally unstaffed; they can range from converted former railway stations to little more than a bus stop.

A common feature of many light rail systems, particularly those which feature street running, is that they are more integrated into the urban environment than conventional railways. In particular, stops can be designed to be a part of the communities they serve rather than being physically separated from them. This design approach impacts on public awareness and passenger perception and can make people more likely to consider travelling on them.

Light rail systems almost universally feature electric power, although there are a very small number of diesel light rail vehicles. Tram-train, a modern concept which has been trialled in Germany, features hybrid vehicles which travel into a city on main line railway tracks, under diesel power if necessary, before switching to tram tracks and electric power for the journey through the city centre.

Difference between trams and light rail

Light rail is a relatively modern term, and can be applied to quite a broad spectrum of systems. Virtually every tram system can be considered as light rail, but only those light rail systems which feature street running can be called trams. It could be said that as light rail is a modern term, only modern systems could be called light rail; however, older tramways still incorporate many of the features of modern light rail systems, and many have also been progressively modernised so that they are very similar to more recently constructed systems.

Metro

Some light rail systems are referred to as 'Metros'. 'Metro' is a term which can be used to describe a high-frequency inter- or intra-urban railway system, which is entirely or largely separate from other main line railway operations. Metro systems often, but not always, feature sections of underground railway and underground stations.

Metros can use either conventional heavy rail technology (heavy metro) or modern light rail technology (light metro). An example in Britain of heavy metro would be the London Underground; examples in Britain of light metro are the Tyne and Wear Metro and the Docklands Light Railway.

⇨ The above information is reprinted with kind permission from TheTrams.co.uk. Visit www.thetrams.co.uk for more information.

THE TRAMS

Transport secretary unveils high-speed rail plans

Transport Secretary Philip Hammond says the Government will consult on building a network incorporating high-speed corridors from the West Midlands to both Manchester and Leeds.

By Hélène Mulholland

Philip Hammond, the Transport Secretary, vowed today to make high-speed rail the 'mode of choice' for the travelling public as he unveiled plans to take fast trains north of Birmingham to Leeds and Manchester.

Hammond outlined the strategic project as demonstrators opposed to the building of the high-speed rail link from London to Birmingham prepared to stage a protest close to the conference centre in Birmingham where the party conference is being held.

An extra £800m is to be pumped into Britain's new high-speed rail network as Tory MPs threaten to rebel against plans to drive the line through the picturesque Chilterns

The *Guardian* reported today that an extra £800m is to be pumped into Britain's new high-speed rail network as Tory MPs threaten to rebel against plans to drive the line through the picturesque Chilterns.

In contrast to Margaret Thatcher, who insisted the Channel Tunnel had to be built with private capital, the Tories are expected to declare that the state will bear the burden of funding the network.

Hammond told delegates at the Tory conference in Birmingham that the Government had set its sights further north than Birmingham, and would consult early next year on building a Y-shaped network incorporating separate corridors from the West Midlands to connect high-speed rail to both Manchester and Leeds.

North of Birmingham, there would be one corridor direct to Manchester, which would then connect to the West Coast Main Line, and the other would go via the East Midlands and South Yorkshire – with stations in both areas – before connecting to the East Coast Main Line north of Leeds.

Hammond told delegates the Government had eschewed an alternative network across the Pennines because the Y route would provide fast journey times to Leeds and north-eastern England and serve additional areas in the East Midlands and South Yorkshire.

The scheme, he said, was a strategic project 'that will make rail the mode of choice for most inter-city journeys within the UK, and for many beyond'.

He said the Chancellor's undertaking that he would support growth boosted the Government's commitment to a high-speed rail network that would change the social and economic geography of Britain.

'Connecting our great population centres and our international gateways, transforming the way Britain works as profoundly as the coming of the original railways did in the mid-19th century.'

He also tackled rail fares, claiming that Britain has one of the most expensive railways in the developed world.

'This is unfair on passengers, and unaffordable for the taxpayer, and with public subsidy running at £5.5bn a year, this has to change,' he said.

He said Network Rail, train operators, the regulator and unions, as well as the Government, needed to change the way they worked together to drive out costs and drive up efficiency while maintaining an 'enviable' safety record.

Turning on tube unions, engaged today on a 24-hour strike in protest over job cuts and safety fears, Hammond sent a message to London Underground workers who thought themselves exempt from change: 'Let me tell them straight: they are not. All our railways have to modernise.'

He threw down the gauntlet to Ed Miliband, the new Labour party leader, to 'come clean' on his position on the 'hugely disruptive and pointless strikes'.

'Just as Ed Miliband has failed to spell out how he would tackle our huge budget deficit, he is also failing to come clean on what he thinks about these hugely disruptive and pointless tube strikes.

'Now he must answer two questions: does he condemn these pointless strikes that are causing disruption to Londoners, and will he encourage underground workers to cross picket lines and keep our capital city moving?'

THE GUARDIAN

Hammond also signalled a two-year suspension of the M4 bus lane – a 3.5-mile stretch of road that starts just after Heathrow airport and runs to the Chiswick flyover on the London-bound section of the motorway.

Hammond told delegates that nothing was more symbolic of Labour's indiscriminate war on motorists.

He said he would 'spoil' the retirement of Lord Prescott, the former deputy prime minister who initiated the scheme, by announcing that the bus lane would be suspended from Christmas Eve this year until the Olympics in the summer of 2012.

'Once the Olympics are over, my intention is to scrap it permanently: shortening average journey times, reducing congestion, restoring a sense of fairness, consigning to the dustbin of history this hated symbol of the Prescott era,' Hammond said.

4 October 2010

High-speed rail misses the point

Billions for rail but what for roads?

A new high-speed rail line costing taxpayers tens of billions of pounds will do nothing to improve the daily journeys of the vast majority of the country's travelling public.

The proposed north–south link also fails to deliver the climate change benefits and reduced road congestion many people hoped for and it offers significantly less value for money than most road schemes.

Commenting on today's release of the HS2 report, Professor Stephen Glaister, director of the RAC Foundation, said:

'Given that a new line won't open until at least 2025, what are our politicians going to do about the capacity crisis we face across the road and rail networks in the next 15 years as the population grows and the economy recovers? More than 90% of daily trips take place on already congested roads and lavishing billions of pounds on a high-speed rail service to benefit the wealthy few who will use the service is not going to change that reality.

'Looked at in isolation this scheme has some merit, with shorter journey times and less crowding for rail passengers going to and from the Midlands. But in the context of this country's huge transport and public funding problems it makes much less sense. It will cost vast amounts of taxpayers' money and only benefit a small number of higher-income passengers. Those who support high-speed rail must, if they are consistent, also support a major increase in public investment in our roads infrastructure.

'For most people, most of the time, the car is public transport, and policy makers must recognise this.'

11 March 2010

⇨ The above information is reprinted with kind permission from the RAC Foundation. Visit www.racfoundation.org for more information.

High speed, high time: the business case for high-speed rail

The UK's railway network is operating near capacity. Passenger numbers continue to increase, yet investment has failed to keep up, resulting in delays and creeping inefficiency.

Congestion on our infrastructure networks already costs British business £23.2 billion every year. Although the network has made huge strides recently with upgrades such as that on the West Coast Main Line and the opening of the UK's first high-speed railway line linking London to Paris, the network is still largely based on its Victorian foundations, with limited scope for further modernisation.

The time has come to take a new look at our railways and to take a view beyond the existing network. A new generation of trains and infrastructure have largely passed the UK by, whereas our continental neighbours have invested heavily in new high-speed networks. France now has a high-speed rail network totalling 1,700 kilometres while Spain, which only began its network in 1992, will have a network totalling 7,000 kilometres by 2010 and is predicted to extend this to 10,000 kilometres by 2020. The UK, on the other hand, has only 108 kilometres.

With public debt standing at almost 60% of GDP and rising, the Government must prioritise where it spends its dwindling resources. Infrastructure, so vital to the economic vitality of the country, will have to compete with other services. A new high-speed rail network might appear expensive, with cost projections reaching upwards of £30 billion, but the railways are a key element of our national infrastructure, linking businesses to labour and markets and contributing significantly to national economic productivity and growth. High-speed rail will contribute significantly to our future economic potential.

Long-term investment, by its very nature, requires early planning. The economic benefits of a high-speed network linking all the major cities will generate revenues and benefits worth almost £55 billion. The Government has predicted that capacity on the current network will be exhausted by 2024. It is therefore imperative that we put in place the foundations for new high-speed lines now so that we are well prepared for the future.

Current issues

The renaissance of the railways has been impressive. Over the last decade passenger numbers have increased by 50% and rail freight by 40%. A total of 49 billion passenger kilometres were travelled on the rail network in 2007/08, an increase of 41% compared to a decade earlier. The growth in rail usage has advanced at such speed that current capacity on the network will be exhausted by 2024, even taking into account planned and anticipated enhancements such as Crossrail and electrification.

BRITISH CHAMBER OF COMMERCE

The railways are a key element of our transport infrastructure, impacting hugely on the development of the regions by increasing connectivity and driving long-term economic growth. With projected population growth forecasts adding to pressures, passenger demand is forecast to grow by a further 73% by 2030. Constraints on the railway limit connectivity and competition, and result in higher prices and increased costs. This is a scenario that business simply cannot afford. More capacity is urgently needed to meet current demand and support future economic growth.

The success of the UK's only high-speed rail line from the continent to London has spurred debate over new high-speed rail infrastructure in the UK

In order to focus on long-term solutions the Government set up the National Networks Strategy Group, which in turn created HS2, a development company to outline the case for a new high-speed rail network. This is a step in the right direction, but a new network will take at least a decade to build. With capacity already constrained and the business case suggesting a cost:benefit ratio of 3.5:1, it is vital the decision to go ahead with additional high-speed lines is taken as quickly as possible.

High Speed 1

The success of the UK's only high-speed rail line from the continent to London has spurred debate over new high-speed rail infrastructure in the UK. Over the past few months both Network Rail and Greengauge21 have released reports proposing new high-speed rail lines. Whereas Network Rail's report proposes new lines in response to the capacity needs of the current network, the Greengauge report goes one step further and outlines the business case for a fully comprehensive network running up both the east and west coasts of the country. In December of this year the Government, via HS2, will announce its preferred route to the West Midlands; the first stage of a real project to build high-speed rail from London to Birmingham.

High Speed 1 (HS1), opened in 2003, brought about a 20-minute reduction in journey time that resulted in a 30% increase in passenger numbers. On completion of the final section in November 2007, Eurostar saw a 21% jump in patronage over the three month period January–March 2008. HS1 is set to deliver over £17 billion in economic benefits, against a cost of £7.3 billion. Journey times on the route have fallen significantly and now link London to Paris and Brussels in a little over two hours. The major benefit of HS1 will be the regeneration

it will bring to three London sites at Stratford, Ebbsfleet and King's Cross, as well as the wider development impacts across Kent. The line will also relieve capacity constraints on central London employment growth and boost housing demand and regeneration in the region. With the introduction of domestic services on the line in December 2009, high-speed rail is here to stay.

High-speed rail – a UK network

The construction of a new high-speed network in the UK will dramatically cut journey times between London, the Midlands, the North and Scotland. Travelling at speeds of up to 200 mph, the distance between London and Scotland could be covered in less than three hours. Such a reduction in journey times will have a huge knock-on effect on productivity, and will present a huge incentive over other forms of transport to both business and leisure travellers.

'For the future, we need to assess the relative merits of building new lines rather than highly disruptive and expensive major upgrades of existing lines. If the cost of disruption is fully taken into account, I suspect it is by no means clear that ostensibly lower price upgrades are always better value than new high-speed lines.'

(Lord Adonis, Secretary of State for Transport, 2009)

High-speed rail offers significant benefits beyond just time savings. It will dramatically increase capacity. High-speed trains are significantly bigger than standard rolling stock, and due to their superior acceleration and higher speeds, more services can be accommodated on one line. In comparison to road travel, a high-speed rail line would have 50% more capacity than the M1 or M6 motorways and achieve journeys in a third of the time possible by road. Further, recent technological progression, in the form of the AGV (Automotrice à Grande Vitesse), means that carriages can be upgraded to double-decker train sets, allowing more passengers to travel at faster speeds and greater frequencies.

Because any new high-speed rail infrastructure will be separate from the existing railway system, it will not negatively impact upon the existing network during construction. A dedicated high-speed network will also free up capacity on existing routes by allowing the conventional network to be utilised for more intensive local passenger and freight services. Cities or towns on the current network that have lost direct connections could see them reinstated, and local commuter services, critical to many businesses and their employees, could be increased. Rail freight, which currently struggles to compete with road transport, will be able to offer more flexible and cost-effective operations. By releasing capacity for freight and local services, it is expected that a shift from road to rail will become vastly more feasible.

As with HS1, the key economic driver of high-speed rail will be the associated agglomeration benefits that such a network will provide, not only to the cities that it serves, but to their wider areas. Greater connectivity, provided by faster and more frequent rail services, will bring businesses closer together. As the reach of businesses increases, production costs will fall as companies are able to access more competing suppliers and a wider pool of labour. Such productivity benefits will also encourage more businesses to locate in or around these areas, which could further increase gains.

High-speed rail could also offer significant environmental benefits, especially if it reduces domestic aviation demand. New and more efficient high-speed trains emit significantly less carbon per passenger than the equivalent trip by air. This is further reduced if the energy source is decarbonised. As a result, high-speed rail should be a key driver in the Government's target to reduce carbon emissions from the transport sector by 14% over the next decade.

However, for high-speed rail to truly benefit the UK, the country requires a network that reaches both North to South and East to West. Whilst there appears to be a growing political consensus over the need for a North–South line, there is a strong and growing economic case for an East–West route too. Linking the North West and North East could add a further 40% in economic benefits to the North by enhancing region-to-region and city-to-city connectivity.

Conclusion

British businesses and the Chamber of Commerce Network believe the case for high-speed rail is clear. As an initial step, the new National Planning Policy Statements resulting from the Planning Act 2008 must call for the identification, protection and preservation of potential paths for a high-speed rail network and its associated stations. HS2 must be instructed to report on the case for a national network once it sets out a path for the line to the West Midlands. High-speed rail in the UK must be planned as a national network.

The construction of a new high-speed network in the UK will dramatically cut journey times between London, the Midlands, the North and Scotland

The business community is pleased that the main political parties have come together on the need for high-speed rail. We support the Government's ongoing work via HS2, and also the Conservatives' and Liberal Democrats' enthusiastic backing, but we disagree with the belief that a new high-speed network should be at the expense of further investment in aviation. While we fully expect high-speed trains to compete with air on domestic routes, we believe there will continue to be a strong role for aviation, especially for business connections. High-speed rail will also create additional demand to Heathrow and the regional airports. As the UK's only hub airport, Heathrow will become a destination in its own right on the network as businesses and leisure travellers seek access to global markets and destinations.

The case for high-speed rail has been stated by Chambers of Commerce, environmental and business groups as well as the main political parties. It is imperative that following the publication of this report the recommendations are taken forward and planning for the UK's high-speed network begins immediately with construction commencing as soon as possible.
November 2009

⇨ The above information is an extract from the British Chamber of Commerce's report *High speed, high time: the business case for high speed rail*, and is reprinted with permission. Visit www.britishchambers.org.uk for more information.

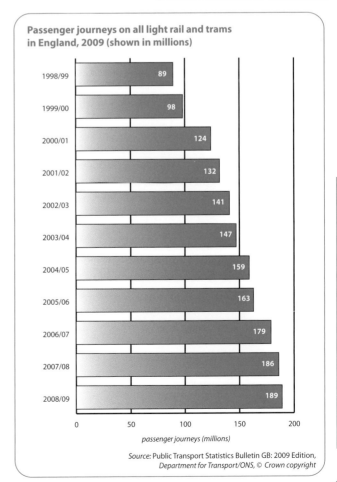

Passenger journeys on all light rail and trams in England, 2009 (shown in millions)

Year	Passenger journeys (millions)
1998/99	89
1999/00	98
2000/01	124
2001/02	132
2002/03	141
2003/04	147
2004/05	159
2005/06	163
2006/07	179
2007/08	186
2008/09	189

passenger journeys (millions)

Source: Public Transport Statistics Bulletin GB: 2009 Edition, *Department for Transport/ONS, © Crown copyright*

BRITISH CHAMBER OF COMMERCE

⇨ The more we use cars, the more the air becomes polluted. Exhaust fumes contain carbon monoxide, oxides of nitrogen, volatile organic compounds and particulates, all of which are harmful to health when released into the atmosphere. (Page 1)

⇨ Surveys show that over half of all primary pupils live within a mile of their school, yet one-third are driven there. (page 2)

⇨ Just under a quarter of adults said that congestion was a problem for the majority of their journeys, a similar level to two years ago but more than the proportion reported last year. (page 5)

⇨ Modern 'road tax' – Vehicle Excise Duty – goes into general taxation. Roads are either paid for from council tax (in the case of smaller, local road schemes) or general taxation (for larger, regional and national schemes). Pedestrians and cyclists therefore contribute just as much towards the cost of road building and maintenance as drivers. (page 7)

⇨ A British truck doing about 100,000 miles a year contributes £30,000 in fuel duty to the UK Treasury. (page 10)

⇨ Buy a new petrol car today for £12,000 and, even if you don't drive a single mile, the first year of ownership will cost you £2,176 in depreciation, road tax and insurance, according to the AA. (page 11)

⇨ Between 2008–09 the number of road deaths fell for almost all types of road user, with a fall of 16% for car occupants, 13% for pedestrians, 10% for pedal cyclists and 4% for motorcyclists. (page 12)

⇨ Transport accounts for around a third of all final energy consumption in the EEA member countries and for more than a fifth of greenhouse gas emissions. (page 14)

⇨ More and more school runs are done by car even though there are other (greener) ways. Transport is 17% of the carbon footprint of the average school or college. (page 19)

⇨ If cycling on the roads at night or in poor visibility, it's a legal requirement for the bike to have: a white front light; a red rear light; a red rear reflector; amber pedal reflectors on the front and rear of each pedal. (page 21)

⇨ Among 32 EEA countries, only Germany and Sweden are on track to meet their 2010 indicative targets for biofuels use. (page 22)

⇨ According to government figures, car traffic has increased some 15% in the last ten years, with congestion estimated to cost some £10 billion per year in English urban areas. (page 23)

⇨ Electric public transport is beginning to prove itself as more than an environmental alternative to diesel vehicles; in fact, it may actually be more suited to the role the vehicle performs. (page 28)

⇨ Light rail has been developed in Manchester, Nottingham, the West Midlands, Tyne and Wear and Sheffield. Light rail development in many large towns and cities in France has demonstrated how high profile infrastructure can help to regenerate cities and hugely improve image and liveability. (page 30)

⇨ A guided busway is usually a dedicated, bus-only route with buses running on a purpose-built track. The bus is guided along the route so that steering is automatically controlled and, like a tram, the vehicle follows a set path. (page 32)

⇨ An extra £800m is to be pumped into Britain's new high-speed rail network. (page 35)

⇨ The construction of a new high-speed network in the UK will dramatically cut journey times between London, the Midlands, the North and Scotland. Travelling at speeds of up to 200mph, the distance between London and Scotland could be covered in less than three hours. (page 38)

Car club

A car share organisation which allows customers to use vehicles as and when they require them, without bearing the cost of buying and running a car of their own. This is an economical and environmentally-friendly way to gain regular access to a car. Customers must cover their own fuel charges and will also be asked to pay a membership fee, allowing them access to one of the club's fleet of vehicles when required. Car clubs are becoming increasingly popular among commuters, especially in urban areas.

Commute

A journey between work and home, made on a regular basis. Someone who regularly travels a set distance to their place of work is known as a commuter.

Congestion

When a large number of vehicles build up on any one stretch of road, causing very slow-moving or stationary traffic, the road is said to be congested. As most people in the UK now own and drive vehicles, congestion is becoming increasingly problematic.

The Congestion Charge

The Congestion Charge is a toll which motorists are required to pay in order to drive within the central London Congestion Charge Zone (CCZ). The controversial fee was introduced in 2003 with the aim of reducing congestion in the city centre. Cameras register the number plate of each vehicle as it enters the CCZ, and fines are imposed if the charge is not paid. There are some exemptions from the charge. It has been reported that due to the 'C-charge' (as it is known), traffic levels in the zone have dropped by around 20%

Electric car

This type of vehicle is fuelled by electricity, which can be recharged at specially-designed charging points. Electric vehicles are considered a green alternative to petrol- or diesel-engine cars, as they have no tail pipe emissions and are therefore less damaging to the environment. A 2008 study by the Department for Business Enterprise and Regulatory Reform predicted that electric vehicles could cut carbon dioxide and greenhouse gas emissions by at least 40%. Electric vehicles are still an emerging technology, but they are expected to have a big impact on the future of automobile production.

Emissions

Emissions are the exhaust fumes that are released from vehicles as they burn fuel. They are damaging to both the environment and people's health, containing, among other chemicals and greenhouse gases, carbon dioxide and carbon monoxide.

High-speed rail

High-speed rail is a relatively new form of transport: a passenger rail service that is able to travel at much greater speeds than traditional trains. High-speed trains travel via direct routes at speeds of around 120–160 miles per hour.

Speed camera

A camera positioned on the side of the road which can measure the speed of vehicles. These devices are used to enforce speed limits: if a camera records the number plate of a vehicle which is exceeding the speed limit, the driver will be fined and/or have points added to their driving licence.

Road tax

A tax that all road users are required to pay in order to own and run a vehicle. It is against the law to drive an untaxed vehicle on the road. The amount of tax levied is based on the size and type of the vehicle. Modern 'road tax' – Vehicle Excise Duty – goes into general taxation.

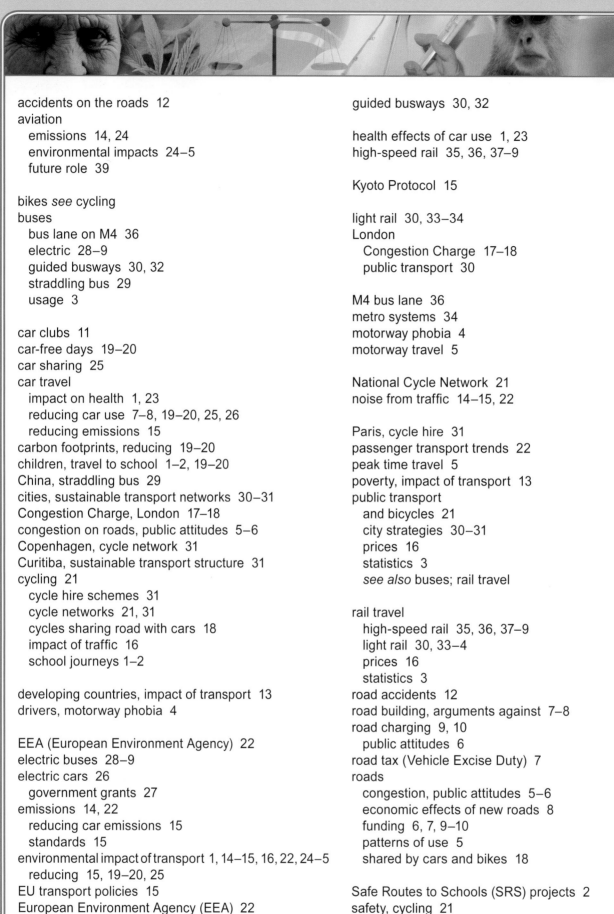

ACKNOWLEDGEMENTS

The publisher is grateful for permission to reproduce the following material.

While every care has been taken to trace and acknowledge copyright, the publisher tenders its apology for any accidental infringement or where copyright has proved untraceable. The publisher would be pleased to come to a suitable arrangement in any such case with the rightful owner.

Chapter One: Transport Trends

Transport, © Keep Britain Tidy, *Use of public transport,* © Crown copyright is reproduced the permission of Her Majesty's Stationery Office, *Motorway phobia,* © Automobile Association, *Public attitudes towards road congestion,* © Crown copyright is reproduced with the permission of Her Majesty's Stationery Office, *The facts about road building,* © Campaign for Better Transport, *Governing and paying for England's roads,* © RAC Foundation, *The road ahead: charging forward,* © Guardian News and Media Group 2010, *Can't afford to run a car?,* © 2010 Associated Newspapers Ltd, *Road deaths fall to 2,222 in 2009,* © Automobile Association, *Transport and global poverty,* © Practical Action.

Chapter Two: Transport and Environment

Transport and the energy crisis, © European Environment Agency, *Car travel,* © carbonfootprint.com, *How heavy traffic harms us,* © Campaign for Better Transport, *Congestion Charge,* © TheSite.org, *Cyclists and motorists do not want to share road, report finds,* © Telegraph Media Group Limited 2010, *Get moving!,* © People and Planet, *Travelling by bike,* © TheSite.org, *Is Europe's transport getting greener? Partly,* © European Environment Agency, *Investment in smarter travel means better health for all,* © Sustrans 2010, www.sustrans.org.uk, *Transport: the way to go,* © Friends of the Earth, *Do governments dream of electric cars?,* ©

Sustrans 2010, www.sustrans.org.uk, *UK electric car grant scheme 'cut by 80%',* © Guardian News and Media Limited 2010, *Electric buses: green public transport or THE public transport?* © Enviro News and Business, *Giant bus which drives over cars planned in China,* © Telegraph Media Group Limited 2010, *Developing city-scale sustainable transport networks,* © CABE/ Urban Practitioners, *Guided busways: frequently asked questions,* © Britpave, *What is a tram?,* © TheTrams. co.uk, *Transport secretary unveils high-speed rail plans,* © Guardian News and Media Limited 2010, *High-speed rail misses the point,* © RAC Foundation, *High speed, high time: the business case for high-speed rail,* © British Chamber of Commerce.

Illustrations

Pages 1, 12, 18, 26, 34: Don Hatcher; pages 2, 19: Bev Aisbett; pages 5, 14, 33, 36: Simon Kneebone; pages 23, 30, 37: Angelo Madrid.

Cover photography

Left: © Mateusz Kapciak. Centre: © Anthony Shapley. Right: © Mattox.

Additional acknowledgements

Research and additional editorial by Carolyn Kirby on behalf of Independence.

And with thanks to the Independence team: Mary Chapman, Sandra Dennis and Jan Sunderland.

Lisa Firth
Cambridge
January, 2011

ASSIGNMENTS

The following tasks aim to help you think through the issues surrounding the sustainable transport debate and provide a better understanding of the topic.

1 Using the figures given in the *Motorway fact file* on page 4, construct two bar graphs which show the differences in motorway driving confidence. One should show the results by gender, the other should display them by age group.

2 Choose one of the myths discussed in the article *The facts about road building* which starts on pages 7–8. Carry out your own research and use your findings to construct a counter-argument to that put forward by the author of this piece. You may find useful information in newspapers, on blogs and on lobby group websites. Try to write concisely and persuasively, justifying your arguments with valid reasons and statistics.

3 Read the article called *Can't afford to run a car?* which starts on page 11. Imagine you work for Streetcar and you are giving a presentation to representatives of the Department for Transport. You are trying to persuade them that they should promote your business, on the basis that your car-share scheme reduces pollution and congestion. You will need to explain how the car club works, the costs involved and the benefits that it brings to society. Prepare a ten-minute 'sales pitch' in small groups, and be prepared to answer questions from the rest of the class at the end of your pitch.

4 Read *Transport and global poverty* on page 13, then visit Practical Action's website at www.practicalaction. org. Use the website to find out about the impact transport, or lack of it, has on developing communities around the world and about Practical Action's work in this area. Then use your findings to devise a fundraising scheme which would help raise money for the charity, as well as awareness of their work among the public.

5 Using some of the suggestions from *Car travel* on page 15, record a short, memorable radio advert, advising drivers on how they can reduce their emissions. Think carefully about persuasive techniques you might use – will you make your ad funny or serious? Will you try to grab their attention with a shocking fact? Or with a light-hearted catchphrase or catchy jingle? Be adventurous!

6 Read the case studies on page 16 in *How heavy traffic harms us*. Choose one of the personal stories and write a letter from the viewpoint of that individual to their local council, airing their transport grievances and asking what action will be taken.

7 Read *Cyclists and motorists do not want to share road, report finds* on page 18. Divide into two groups, with one group representing 'motorists' and one group representing 'cyclists', and stage a debate between the two groups about how the road should be used.

8 Using online newspaper archives, do some research into electric cars and their role in the future of transport. In particular, look for articles which cover the debate over the viability of developing electric cars as the 'next big thing'. Write a report on your findings.

9 The article on page 29 describes an idea for a new mode of transport designed to ease congestion. In groups of four, brainstorm the problems and challenges associated with current modes of transport: for example, road congestion and rail prices. Based on the issues that you have identified, devise a new mode of transport to help address one of these issues. Draw a diagram of your invention and provide details on how expensive it would be to run, whether it would be suited to city transport or long distances and any associated environmental benefits.

10 Imagine that a new guided busway has been built in your local town. Create an eye-catching poster advertising the service, encouraging people to use the busway instead of driving. You can use the information on page 32, *Guided busways: frequently asked questions*, to help you.

11 Carry out a research project into transport in your area. First of all, make a list of all the modes of transport that are available to your local community. Then conduct a survey among community members to establish which methods are the most popular. You could also contact influential community members for more information on the transport situation: a local councillor, for example. Summarise your findings in a report.

12 The articles on pages 35 to 39 give different opinions on the benefits of a new high-speed rail system in Britain. Summarise each argument, for and against, in two short paragraphs. Which do you agree with?

13 Use resources available on the Internet to work out your carbon footprint. Is the result what you expected? Compare your answer with other students in your class.